RISE AND REBUILD:
A GUIDE TO OVERCOMING ADVERSITY

DISCOVER THE POWER OF NEHEMIAH'S EXAMPLE TO REBUILD YOUR LIFE AND FULFILL YOUR PURPOSE

Robert Stearns

FOREWORD BY
Samuel Rodriguez

DEDICATION

For the past 25 years, as I have tried to Rise and Rebuild my personal life and impact the world around me, I have been accompanied on this journey by an incredible couple. Stephen and Veronica Jenks wake up - every day - and intentionally live for God's Kingdom. When I think of the famous phrase "My Utmost for His Highest" (Oswald Chambers), I think of them.

Stephen and Veronica "Rise" every day and help "Rebuild" our world, especially the world of their amazing children, Abigail and Shane.

I dedicate this work to Stephen and Veronica and their beautiful family.

SPECIAL ACKNOWLEDGMENT

For more than 20 years, Aaron Derstine has been my friend and co-journeyer on the road to Zion. He is an amazing student of the Bible and a spiritual leader. He has been my research assistant and writing partner on several of my writing projects, including this one. This book is as much his as mine, and I am very grateful to him.

ENDORSEMENTS

The Scriptural ministry of the apostle is one of a master builder (1 Cor. 3:10). They are to be, alongside the prophets, the foundation of the church (Eph. 2:20) and those who direct the execution of its Kingdom mandate upon the earth.

Bishop Robert Stearns walks in a global office of the Apostle, carrying within him the architectural vision and blueprints of this glorious building of the church both inwardly in the lives of people and outwardly through raising them up as equipped Kingdom Ambassadors (2 Cor. 5:20). In "Rise and Rebuild," Bishop Robert begins to release these revolutionary blueprints to the body of Christ.

Walking alongside Bishop Robert as both Spiritual Son and Successor to Tommy and Spiritual brother and mentor to Aimee, has been the greatest privilege of our lives. We have watched him navigate seemingly insurmountable obstacles, pain, and wrestling and come through not only with victory, but with a depth of the word of the Lord, His presence and glory, and a readiness to bring the global community of faith into an intentional building plan rooted in the ancient pathways (Jer. 6:16-17).

We invite you into this journey with our beloved friend, Bishop Robert, as we "come Home again" and rebuild.

—Bishop Tommy Reid
The Tabernacle Bishop Emeritus
COVNet Bishop

—Pastor Aimee Reid-Sych
The Tabernacle Worship Pastor
COVNet President
United Women Rise President

I am very pleased to highly recommend to you the ministry and the latest book Rise and Rebuild of Bishop Robert Stearns, one of the foremost leaders in the Church today. We are glad to have Bishop Robert as one of the Board members of CGI.

Bishop Robert is making an extraordinary impact around the world, mobilizing support for Israel and a deeper Biblical understanding of the Jewish roots of our faith. In his new book, he guides you through the story of Nehemiah, producing powerful insights that will challenge, teach, and equip you to be an effective wall builder in the Kingdom of God.

—Dr. Younghoon Lee, Senior Pastor
Yoido Full Gospel Church & General Superintendent,
Assemblies of God of Korea

With trowel in one hand and sword in the other, Nehemiah takes on the immense task of rebuilding a broken people. Robert Stearns personalizes the story for every believer in hope and a new beginning.

A must read and worthy addition to your library.

—Rev. A. R. Bernard, Sr.
Christian Cultural Center
New School of Biblical Theology
Commission of Religious Leaders
Sheen Center for Thought and Culture

In his new book "Rise and Rebuild," Bishop Robert Stearns gives you powerful and practical application for living a lifestyle of an overcomer! I have been so enriched and blessed to know and partner with Bishop Robert and his ministry, and I believe you will be greatly strengthened as you read and apply the truths in this book into your own life circumstances.

Our nation needs righteous wall builders like never before, and you are holding in your hands an invitation and opportunity to be part of a mighty move of God in this generation!

—Kathy Branzell
President, National Day of Prayer Task Force

A lot of people are all house and no foundation. Dr. Robert Stearns, in his latest book "Rise and Rebuild," is destined to be the quintessential book to turning wreckage into worship and shambles into success.

As a wise master builder, I encourage you to buy a book for yourself and a box of books for your team. Read it now and reap for years to come!

—Dr. James O. Davis
Founder/President Global Church Network
Greater Orlando, Florida Area
www.GCNW.tv

After a half-century serving the nation of India and building on the promises of God in my beloved homeland, I have seen time and again that the broken people of this world—the poor, the oppressed, the marginalized—are people of great worth and dignity. The broken ones can be great men and women of God and be used to accomplish significant things for Him.

Bishop Stearns' exposition of the life and work of Nehemiah will encourage any reader that they, too, can be image bearers of God in this world. After reading "Rise and Rebuild," followers of Jesus will seek their role in building the Kingdom of God on earth today.

—Rev. Dr. Joseph D'souza
Archbishop/Moderator
Good Shepherd Church of Asia/Middle East

It is with profound admiration and brotherly affection that I put pen to paper in endorsing my dear friend, Bishop Robert Stearns. He is not merely a remarkable influencer and pioneer in his field — he is also an extraordinary individual who, with steadfast determination, is illuminating a new path in the intricate tapestry of Jewish-Christian relations, particularly with regard to the Evangelical Christian embrace of the State of Israel.

Throughout our shared endeavors over many years, the collaboration has been much more than a partnership—it has been a profound spiritual journey that has fostered a genuine appreciation for the sacred task that binds us together. The essence of this holy mission, especially in the world's present state, is all the more poignant, serving as a beacon of unity and understanding between kindred spirits of different faiths.

Bishop Stearns' most recent book, a deeply insightful exploration of the trials and triumphs of Nehemiah, transcends the boundaries of mere text on paper. It is a heartfelt testament, imbued with tangible emotion and irrefutable wisdom, which urges every reader to find their divine calling, and overcome the personal impediments that may obstruct their path to God and His holy word as revealed to us in the words of the Hebrew Scriptures.

Each chapter of this magnificent work has the potential to touch your soul, generating a profound transformation within. I am confident that the illumination Bishop Stearns has poured into these pages will not just inspire, but also empower you to draw deep into your reservoir of potential, unraveling the Divine plan crafted specifically for you. Furthermore, this book can also serve as a conduit, bridging the distance between individuals worldwide who are on a similar journey, seeking their purpose and overcoming their unique challenges by doing it together, and with each other. Through this bond, we can nurture a global community of enlightenment and growth, fostering mutual respect and understanding.

In endorsing Bishop Stearns, I am not just endorsing an esteemed author or a revered religious leader—I am endorsing a noble spirit whose tireless efforts and unflinching dedication to fostering unity is a testament to his extraordinary character. As you embark on this journey through the lens of Nehemiah, under the guidance of Bishop Stearns, prepare to be stirred, challenged, and inspired like never before.

—Rabbi Pini Dunner
Senior Rabbi, YINBH Beverly Hills Synagogue

I have personally witnessed the impressive work of Bishop Robert Stearns, his tireless commitment to work for a better, brighter world, and specifically his bridge-building between Christians and Jews. Israel and the world are the beneficiaries of his inspired efforts.

Bishop Stearns' insightful new book about the life of Nehemiah is a dynamic application of a story from ancient Israel that still speaks with relevance today.

I heartily recommend to you this book and the groundbreaking work of Bishop Stearns in this vital time in history.

—David M. Friedman

Former United States Ambassador to Israel

My friend Bishop Robert Stearns has done it again! Bishop Stearns shows us how to trust the God of the impossible when we face broken dreams and disappointments in this timely book on Nehemiah's life and journey.

This book is inspirational and thought-provoking, allowing the reader to go deeper in self-reflection and move from broken to building! Bishop Stearns' ministry continues to have a significant impact around the world. You don't want to miss out on this transformative read.

—Dr. John-Paul C. Foster

Senior Pastor, Faithful Central Bible Church

Rebuild, raise up, repair, and restore from Isaiah 58:12 were the strong verbs that motivated our restart in 1985, coupled with a daily devotional pursuit of Nehemiah's journal.

Bishop Stearns' book, "Rise and Rebuild: A Guide to Overcoming Adversity," could have very well been our roadmap, had it been available. He is a seasoned and gifted communicator whose life and ministry underscore the message.

—Bishop Joseph L. Garlington
Presiding Bishop of Reconciliation Ministries

Over the last number of years, I have had the honor of working alongside and personally experiencing the impact of Bishop Robert Stearns and Eagles' Wings, and I can say unequivocally that he is a leader who is changing the landscape of interfaith relations, particularly in advancing Christian support for Israel.

In this new book inspired by the biblical account of Nehemiah, he ties together our two faith communities for the changing of individual lives and for strategic purpose through key scriptural lessons. This is a superbly done and highly relatable manuscript that will greatly benefit you on your journey of faith.

—Mark Gerson
Entrepreneur, Philanthropist, and Author of the best-selling book *The Telling: How Judaism's Essential Book Reveals the Meaning of Life*

I was blessed to have met Robert many years ago. His faithful work through Eagles' Wings has pioneered wonderful support for Israel which is near and dear to my heart.

As you read Robert's book "Rise and Rebuild" from the story of Nehemiah, I know you will be filled with new courage to overcome obstacles and live with a deeper hope that will make a tangible difference for you and all those you love and whose lives you touch.

—Kathie Lee Gifford
Former co-host of NBC's TODAY and Author of NYT
bestseller *The Rock, The Road & The Rabbi* and
The God of The Way

Bishop Robert Stearns not only imparts valuable knowledge through this book, but also shares profound revelation and personal experience that will resonate with the reader's own journey. In a time when so many people are hurt and broken, without knowing how to fix themselves, this book is set to bring hope and restoration to those in need. There is no doubt that this book carries a message that will not only cause people to be healed but will help others to let go of the past and be propelled towards their destiny.

—Teófilo Hayashi
Senior Leader of Zion Church
Leader and Founder of Dunamis Movement

FOREWORD

In every generation, I believe that God has His "Generals" who are appointed to stand at the crossroads of history, to survey what needs to be done, and to mobilize the people of God to action. From ancient Israel to the 21ˢᵗ century, this narrative has never changed, because God Himself never changes and His purpose to raise up a people for Himself, who live, breathe, and act like Him has never wavered.

When I met Bishop Robert Stearns a few decades ago, I immediately knew I had met a dynamic leader to whom I was going to be connected for a long time. Those of us who know Robert Stearns know that he literally wakes up daily and works to make our world a better, more equitable, just, and meaningful place for all people. His passion and zeal to make a difference inspire me, and to this day I am honored to call Robert Stearns my personal friend.

I have been so impacted by Bishop Robert's tireless work on behalf of Israel and the Jewish people around the world, through groundbreaking efforts like the annual Day of Prayer for the Peace of Jerusalem, for which I have the privilege of serving as co-chair with him. And while this book is about so much more than that, Robert's first-hand understanding of the Jewish people and decades of experience in Jewish / Christian dialogue serve as the unmistakable backdrop for his insights in his powerful book *Rise and Rebuild.*

The biblical character Nehemiah, one of those mighty generals of God and the central figure of this book, is a profound example of determination, faith, courage, and covenant faithfulness. His "never-take-no-for-an-answer" attitude set the stage for a massive moment in Israel's history through the rebuilding of the walls of Jerusalem.

Nehemiah is known for being the pioneer, the leader of the charge to rebuild God's Holy City, in a time filled with many naysayers. He defied the odds by internalizing the promises of God spoken to his people the Jews and by doing something about it.

As my brother Robert so aptly shares, Nehemiah first had to have a personal experience with Israel's God, encountering His faithfulness and knowing Him to be the One who had the power to rebuild Broken Places. Nehemiah's mission was God's mission – which is why no amount of opposition could derail it. But Nehemiah had a choice to make, each and every day that he walked through the arduous and at times exhausting process of seeing his God do the impossible.

Because Nehemiah chose well and led the people well, we are still here today talking about it—and the people of Israel have continued in their perpetual bond to their homeland, even when being dispersed to the nations before their nation was reborn centuries later.

Make no mistake, our God is a God of miracles—but He is also looking for those who will partner with Him to see those epic miracles take place in the here and now.

This book is not an empty historical study. It is a battle guide to stand in the Broken Places of today's culture and the Broken Places of our own lives and declare, "I serve the God of Nehemiah, the One who can rebuild broken-down walls!" It's going to take tangible work to live like this; but as they say, nothing worth doing was ever easy. The price is high, but the rewards are limitless.

I don't know about you, but I want "in" on that kind of lifestyle in this enormously crucial hour. The fact that you are reading this book right now is a strong indication that you are the kind of person who is not satisfied by simply keeping the status quo. If you're hungry for more – to restore, to advance, to rebuild – then you are about to be equipped in a life-defining way as you read the following pages.

I can't think of anyone more suited to lead us through this process of timely discovery than Bishop Robert Stearns. Without a doubt, he is one of the Nehemiah's that God has raised up in this generation, bridging the gap between Jew and Gentile and bringing us back to the ancient covenants instituted by the God of Israel. You are in the right place and at the right time… and you picked up the right battle guide.

Where evil and chaos have ripped society apart and torn righteous walls down, let's rise up and rebuild. If we don't do it, who will?

Join me and my friend Robert on the adventure of a lifetime… a 900-mile trek with Nehemiah through the desert, through adversity, through the pain of the past, and into the promise of the future. The world will never be the same because of your "yes" to the God of Nehemiah.

Let's become wall builders together!

—Rev. Samuel Rodriguez
Senior Pastor, New Season Church, Sacramento, CA
President, National Hispanic Christian Leadership Conference
(NHCLC)

TABLE OF CONTENTS

PREFACE

L ately, I've been struck by the overwhelming, all-pervasive power of story. We are surrounded by, formed by, carried by, and compelled by stories. Stories have far more power in our lives than we consciously realize.

Family stories, national stories, fables, folklore, religious stories—stories surround us from our very earliest consciousness. They are with us in the last season of our lives, when we especially reflect on the stories of our past.

The farther we are removed from these stories in time, what seems to emerge as important is not the exact and precise details of the story but rather the overarching theme and "point," which makes the story still relevant to us today. If the story doesn't have a strong, enduring, timeless, and universal message, it tends to fade. The stories that endure are the ones with a lesson worth remembering and relaying to the next generation.

Nehemiah is surely such a story.

All the necessary elements are here to keep us on the edge of our seats. Why Hollywood hasn't told this story yet, I don't know. But maybe they yet will.

I'm honored to retell this story for you. As I did in two of my previous books, "Keepers of the Flame" and "The Cry of Mordecai," I'm attempting to lift the curtain from the most reductive perspective ("Oh yeah—Nehemiah's the guy who rebuilt the walls of Jerusalem") and take us deeper, higher, and broader into a multi-dimensional consideration of this epic tale.

I'm forever grateful for the amazing team without whom I am truly and fully lost and ineffective. The entire immediate and extended 40-plus member unified team of Eagles' Wings and The Tabernacle is such a blessing and inspiration, and I thank each of them for all they do. In particular, Wendy Miller has run my schedule and the details of my life for the past 24 years. I regularly check with her to ask her where I am supposed to be and what I'm supposed to be doing, and somehow she always knows.

My sons, Isaac, Daniel, and Michael, live out the challenges and blessings of having me as their father. It's not always easy on them, and I pray that, somehow, the blessings outweigh the challenges. May you walk in Nehemiah's example and always be lovers of God, servants of mankind, and defenders of Jerusalem, all the days of your life.

Over the last months of finishing this book, five people who are precious to me "graduated to Glory." Each of them touched my life in a profound and enduring way. Each of them shared their stories with me, and part of them lives on in me. I will never, ever forget them. I honor Pastor Jack Hayford, Pastor Al Baun, Billie Ann Smith, Sister Lorraine Minor (widow of the late Dr. David Minor), and Dolly Eleiott. I owe each of them so much and cherish my memories with them.

I pray that we will look deeper into this incredible drama and be renewed in faith, hope, and determination in the personal, communal, and even global aspects of our lives to, like Nehemiah, "Rise and Rebuild."

BROKEN PLACES IN A BROKEN WORLD

To live is to build.

Each of us is building something. We may be building a family, a career, a company, a ministry, a plan for retirement, a relationship. But each of us, consciously or not, is involved in building. We may have a crystal-clear blueprint, or we may just be going by some unspoken, vague, inner idea. But we are building—successfully or unsuccessfully—nonetheless.

In the midst of our building, it is inevitable that we are going to face the pain and disappointment of times and places of brokenness.

We live in a broken world. Each of us can easily point to so many things, in our individual lives, our families, our communities, our nations, our world, that are not "as they should be." These things cause us emotional or physical challenges, pain, frustration, or at times even trauma in some way.

Divorce, a lost or struggling relationship with a child, a bankruptcy in business, a conflict in a house of worship, an inner

> **There are those courageous ones who look at what is but see what could be.**

brokenness that no amount of prayer or time has been able to heal—there is no shortage of places where brokenness becomes evident.

The question for you and me is quite simple.

What are we going to do about it?

What are we going to do, if anything, about the Broken Places?

THE CHOICE OF A LIFETIME

Be clear. You DO have a choice. You can do nothing. You can accept the Broken Places as they are and leave them there. Some (many, in fact!) have decided that trying to repair the Broken Places is too risky, too costly, too dangerous, and the outcome too uncertain. Better to accept things as they are, this line of thinking goes, than to risk losing what little security you have.

But there are those courageous ones who look at what is but see what could be. They see themselves as part of a long line of dreamers and doers who throw themselves into places of breakdown and chaos and decide to become Builders and Repairers. They realize, with full clarity, that they may very well not succeed.

Except—they have redefined success.

Success is not the completion of the goal. Success, for them, is in getting up every day, no matter how tired, how cold, how alone...

and putting themselves to the task again. Success is in the effort. The commitment. The call. The cause.

A year after he left office, former U.S. President Theodore Roosevelt delivered a speech in Paris that was entitled "Citizenship in a Republic," often referred to also as "The Man in the Arena." In this well-known April 1910 address, he stated:

> *It is not the critic who counts; not the man who points out how the strong man stumbles, or where the doer of deeds could have done them better. The credit belongs to the man who is actually in the arena, whose face is marred by dust and sweat and blood; who strives valiantly; who errs, who comes short again and again, because there is no effort without error and shortcoming; but who does actually strive to do the deeds; who knows great enthusiasms, the great devotions; who spends himself in a worthy cause; who at the best knows in the end the triumph of high achievement, and who at the worst, if he fails, at least fails while daring greatly, so that his place shall never be with those cold and timid souls who neither know victory nor defeat.[1]*

The good news is that history shows that Builders and Repairers have a great ally—the person of God Himself. Isaiah prophesied about the Builders. "Those from among you shall build the old waste places; you shall raise up the foundations of many generations; and you shall be called the Repairer of the Breach, the Restorer of Streets to Dwell In" (Isaiah 58:12).

"Those from among you shall build the old waste places; you shall raise up the foundations of many generations; and you shall be called the Repairer of the Breach, the Restorer of Streets to Dwell In."

—Isaiah 58:12

Our God is not afraid of brokenness. Not yours, and not mine. In fact, one could make the case that He actually gravitates towards impossible situations, heartaches, and pain. I like to think it allows Him to "show off" and display His God-ness.

He is the Healer of the brokenhearted (see Psalm 147:3), and in describing the Presence of God that shines into the hearts of all who believe in Him, 2 Corinthians 4:7 says, "But we have this treasure in earthen vessels, that the excellence of the power may be of God and not of us."

Earthen vessels… so easily broken by those who would seek to trample on them. So often marred by the winds and floods of life that beat against the structure. So despairingly shattered by the unexpected tragedies that assail friend and foe alike in this life.

What are your Broken Places today?

I want to dare you to dream. To challenge you to believe. God wants to partner with you in healing your Broken Places, and then in using your life and testimony to help heal Broken Places in our world.

GO TO YOURSELF

In Genesis 12:1, centuries before Nehemiah, God commanded Abram to leave everything that was comfortable to him and step out to make a new home for his family, which was to be in the land of Canaan. The name for the *parsha* (Torah Portion) that begins with this verse is *Lech Lecha*, which in Hebrew means "go to yourself." Before anything else, God's command to Abram was first a challenge to make changes in his life that would affect himself.

As we will see throughout Nehemiah's life story, true leadership only happens when the leader is willing to step forward and break through his or her own process, no matter how painful, before those whom that person is leading.

God is in the business of taking broken things and somehow using them for good. Unfortunately for us, this is much more easily said than experienced. We may never know the meaning, the "why," we had to experience certain things. God might never find it necessary to tell us. And what if He doesn't? What will our response be?

REPAIRING THE WORLD

There is a concept in Judaism that has become a plumb line, a word of direction for me in my life. It is known as *tikkun olam*—or the repairing of the world. Ever since the fall of man—and even

> **Your brokenness does not disqualify you from being used by God. Rather, it can become the very thing that *qualifies* you.**

before, in the vastness of His wisdom—God's desire has been for a people who will participate with Him in His ultimate story of redemption and restoration in the earth. He calls us to join Him in the timeless work of "re-creating" the world that He created as perfectly good.

I invite you to study with me the incredible life of one such Builder and Repairer. Nehemiah has become one of my heroes. His story is epic, but also very relatable.

One of the things I especially love about his story is that there are not any "miraculous" or "supernatural" aspects to his story, as there are in so many other stories in scripture. No angels, no weather-related miracles, no supernatural multiplication of food. In other words, Nehemiah's story, which is epic and some might say has miraculous results, came about through simple but profound human obedience, passion, perseverance, courage, and hard work.

As we discover these life lessons together, I hope you will find with me what I have found to be true: that our brokenness does not disqualify us from being used by God. Rather, it can become the very thing that *qualifies* us. The rubble of our brokenness can produce the building blocks of our beautiful future, the open door towards the unfolding of a glorious destiny that is part of the vast story that God Himself is telling in the earth.

Come with me as we delve into this remarkable biblical story together—the story of Nehemiah.

FOR FURTHER STUDY:

1. What can you identify as an area or multiple areas of deep brokenness in your own life that you know God wants to heal, rebuild, and restore?

_____

_____

_____

_____

_____

2. Name the Hebrew phrase that means "the repairing of the world." What could this concept mean for you when lived out on a daily basis?

_____

_____

_____

_____

_____

_____

3. Do you see yourself as qualified to be used by God? Why or why not?

_____

_____

_____

_____

_____

4. If there was one thing you could build in and through your life, what would it be?

_____

_____

_____

_____

_____

EXILE AND THE BROKEN PLACES

YOUR CONNECTION TO NEHEMIAH'S STORY

"Suffering makes a people greater, and we have suffered much. We had a message to give the world, but we were overwhelmed, and the message was cut off in the middle. In time there will be millions of us—becoming stronger and stronger—and we will complete the message."

– David Ben-Gurion,
First prime minister of the State of Israel[2]

Scripture is filled with stories of unknown heroes and unlikely endings.

Over and again, God rescues His people Israel from the brink of destruction—and more often than not, He uses someone who is unqualified, unusual, or un-esteemed to achieve His purpose.

Chosen by God to be separate and distinct from the other nations, the people of Israel shouldered their weighty calling with the brokenness and frailty that has characterized the condition of

> **Each of us, deeply and innately, longs for home. A place of belonging, of knowing, of safety, of peace.**

humanity throughout history. They were an imperfect people with imperfect leaders, but they were also a people with a Promise.

They were a broken people, but a people whose God was (and is) a Restorer and Rebuilder.

Exile. Brokenness. Two realities that we all relate to.

Each of us, deeply and innately, longs for Home. A place of belonging, of knowing, of safety, of peace. Our own "Jerusalem." But when brokenness enters our lives, through whatever form, an exile occurs. We are "cut off" from Home. We may be in the same physical place we have always been, but it is no longer Home. It is no longer safe. And so, we are no longer our truest selves. This brokenness then extends itself towards those we love most. We become alienated and strangers from those whom we long to love, because the Destroyer has come to cut us off from ourselves, from those we love, and from God Himself.

Those of us who have lived through abusive relationships, whether in childhood or adulthood or both, come to realize that the deepest wound that is inflicted on us is not whatever abuse has happened to our bodies or our minds, but rather a horrible sense of being cut off from any sense of peace, of centeredness, of being able to rest in our Home.

Brokenness and exile go hand in hand. And so Israel's story, over and over, is a story of Returning and Rebuilding. And this is our story, and our invitation.

CONTEXT MATTERS

As we delve into this story, bear with me for a bit of a history lesson. Maybe you are someone who finds dates and historical facts to be tedious or boring—but stay with me for just a few minutes... as we set the stage of the historical backdrop for this remarkable biblical narrative. After we gain some context, we will go back and discover together the inspirational insights from Nehemiah, which I pray will become revelation for you on your own journey.

The book of Nehemiah unfolds on the scene of Israel's Broken Places as they are exiles in captivity in Persia. No strangers to devastation, the people of Israel knew collectively what it was to have their city Jerusalem burned with fire by the Babylonians, and their sons and daughters carried into exile.

Israel had been a united people under the one God. But they became a fractured people of many gods, after the days of King Solomon, when the united kingdom of Israel was split into the northern kingdom of Israel and the southern kingdom of Judah. There would never be a godly king in the North, and only a few in the South merited that description. The northern kingdom fell to Assyria in 722 BC; the southern kingdom, led by a few righteous kings (like Hezekiah and Josiah) who appeared every few generations, endured until it succumbed to Nebuchadnezzar of Babylon in 586 BC.

Isaiah, Jeremiah, Amos, Micah... the company of prophetic voices "crying in the wilderness"... time and again warned the people of Israel and Judah, exhorting them to return with all their hearts to their God, the God of Israel. Calling them to come Home. In cyclical fashion, the people would return, but then, seemingly just as quickly, they would turn away from God once again. At the helm was a litany of wicked kings, interrupted only every few generations by a righteous ruler who would acknowledge the God of Israel once again.

The few among the people whose hearts remained loyal to the God of their fathers were becoming the minority in the land.

Finally, threatened by the intimidation of Babylon, the Israelites appeared to forget altogether who they were, as well as the might of their God, and began the descent into servitude to their enemies.

As early as 597 BC, some of the people of Judah were taken in captivity in Babylon. Under oppression from their enemy, waves of captives were taken in increasing measure. Finally the city of Jerusalem itself was besieged in 587 BC and destroyed by 586 BC. The majority of the people were then taken to the foreign land.

The unimaginable had really happened—devastation as a people and deportation to Babylon.

This was not the way it was supposed to be.

Israel had many stories of victories that were passed down from generation to generation:

- The Red Sea crossing under Moses' leadership

- The battle of Jericho under Joshua

- King David's conquest of Jerusalem

- The building of the glorious temple under Solomon

- God's defeat of the enemy armies when the people under Jehoshaphat went into battle singing praises.

But those miracle stories of Israel with unlikely heroes faded with time and seemed like distant memories… as if the very stories themselves had been buried in the charred rubble of Jerusalem.

GENESIS OF DOUBT

When we are facing our Broken Places, from whatever exile we find ourselves in, these miracle stories (which are meant to encourage us) can at times seem like a cruel mockery. God seems to have provided miracles for others, but where is my miracle?

Where is my breakthrough?

Where is my shalom?

Slowly, we begin to doubt the goodness of God, or at least His goodness to "me." Our hearts shut down, one layer at a time, and we (quietly at first) begin to doubt the goodness of God, the

> **Our hearts shut down, one layer at a time, and we (quietly at first) begin to doubt the goodness of God, the promises of God, and then eventually, even the truth of His existence.**

promises of God, and then eventually, even the truth of His existence.

Would the people of Israel ever return? Jeremiah's prophecy declared that they would be in captivity for 70 years (Jeremiah 25:11-12), but when the people were taken away, that promise was far off into the distant future.

And maybe, just maybe, this was really the end—maybe God would turn His back on them for good this time.

Psalm 137 captures the heart of a people in brokenness as they remembered Home... the glories of David's kingdom, and the glorious city *Yerushalayim* that was at its center:

By the rivers of Babylon, There we sat down, yea, we wept When we remembered Zion. We hung our harps Upon the willows in the midst of it. For there those who carried us away captive asked of us a song, And those who plundered us requested mirth, Saying, "Sing us one of the songs of Zion!"

How shall we sing the Lord's song In a foreign land? If I forget you, O Jerusalem, Let my right hand forget its skill! If I do not remember you, Let my tongue cling to the roof of my mouth— If I do not exalt Jerusalem Above my chief joy.

> ## DID YOU KNOW?
>
> **Where It All Began:** The Fertile Crescent, the Middle East region where ancient civilizations began, has two major rivers at its center: the Tigris and Euphrates. The Euphrates River ran right through Babylon (as scripture says, "*By the rivers of Babylon...*" Psalm 137:1).

HOPE REMEMBERED

Finally, the days came when the prophet Daniel had risen to the forefront as one of God's most seasoned voices in the land of exile. At that time, a faint glimmer of hope appeared. It was the year 539 BC; nearly 60 years after the first captives of Judah were taken.

The Babylonians, with all their might, magnificence, and military domination, fell to the invading Medes and Persians. But the people of Israel remained captives, a type of transferred property from one kingdom to another.

The very next year, however, 538 BC, captives began to return to Judah under the permission granted by Cyrus the Great, the unifier and founder of the Persian Empire. Talk about a change in policy—from the fiery furnace of Nebuchadnezzar the Babylonian to the opportunity of returning home under Cyrus the Persian!

Even so, it was a long road ahead. As the people of Judah would find, going *Home* was very different from going *back*. They had been through fiery trials, and the only way for them to go from that moment was *forward*—straight through the doubts and fears that accompanied a new but extremely daunting beginning in the midst of their Broken Places.

What do we do when we are in exile? When we are overwhelmed by the Broken Places?

What do I want you and I together to do as we encounter this story, which is a story of Return and Rebuilding?

We Remember.

And...

We Hope.

We remember, perhaps not even things that ever have been, but things that *should be*. One of my early mentors, Rabbi Gerald Meister (of blessed memory), would say, "Hope is Remembering things which are Yet to Be."

This is hard and requires great courage. Many of us, so many times, have had our hope deferred, which makes our hearts sick (Proverbs 13:12). But Romans 5:3-5 tells us,

And not only that, but we also glory in tribulations, knowing that tribulation produces perseverance; and perseverance, character; and character, hope. Now hope does not disappoint, because the love of God has been poured out in our hearts by the Holy Spirit who was given to us.

Returning and Rebuilding requires that we Remember in Hope.

So we see that the invitation to return from Exile and to rebuild the Broken Places requires not only remembering, for remembering alone can bring nostalgia at best, and bitterness and cynicism at worst. Returning and Rebuilding requires that we Remember in Hope.

My favorite movie of all time is *The Matrix*. (Anyone with me on that?) As Neo stands in the great battle that is his life, the Architect mocks him:

"Hope. It is the quintessential human delusion. Simultaneously the source of your greatest strength, and your greatest weakness."[3]

As we consider Nehemiah's story and the spiritual, psychological, and practical principles we can learn to Rebuild the Broken Places, I want to let you know now, here at the beginning, that our Return Home will require that we Remember in Hope.

That will likely be painful.

A heart that is shut down knows few tears, but opening ourselves again often requires us to pass through the valley of weeping (Psalm 84:6).

Jeremiah 31:17 describes a period of weeping in Israel's history when God's words of comfort came to His people: "There is hope in your future... that your children shall come back to their own border." This prophecy came not from a joyous place but from a response to the cry of Rachel over her children in exile. God responded to her cry, to her low place, to what seemed to be her loss of Hope. "There IS Hope..." God replies. From this broken place, there is Hope.

We will have to commit ourselves to this Hope, without absolute certainty that we will see the results of our Hope in the way we want or in the time frame we want. The free will of other people is a part of the complicated story. But ultimate victory, ultimate redemption, and our personal healing are not derived from outward circumstances, no matter how much we wish for things to be a certain way in the here and now.

The Jews in exile for almost 2,000 years after 70 AD who prayed, "Next year in Jerusalem," were just as victorious as the Jews who saw this prophetic prayer come true in 1948. Because the victory is in the Hoping. The victory is in the Journey. The victory is in seeing and believing and knowing that God will do all things well, whether we fully see that manifest in our lifetimes or not.

HaTikvah, or "The Hope," the Israeli national anthem, was first composed as a poem by Naphtali Herz Imber in 1877, 71 years before the establishment of the State in 1948.[4] The hope exists long before the answer is near. This is faith.

This is an arduous thing, this living in Hope. I always laugh at unbelievers who say, "Religious faith is a crutch for the weak." True faith, in my opinion, requires incredible courage and strength. To wake up daily and put on faith, put on hope, and put on trust is a decision of strength. But the alternative—to live in doubt, fear, self-protection—what is that? That is existing, not living. That is the path of sad cowardice.

FROM EXILE TO ACTION

Living in their place of exile, mere words and prayers could not turn the fortunes of the people of Judah. If they had sentiment alone with no action to back it up, their Broken Places and exile would remain. So as He had done so many times throughout their history, God looked for a deliverer who would take action on behalf of the people—and this time He chose a man whose very name in Hebrew literally meant "The Comfort of YHWH."

There was nothing extraordinary about the man Nehemiah on the surface. He was not born into nobility or wealth. Though his job brought him (like Esther a few decades before) to the Persian palace, he lived under subjugation and servitude along with the rest of his people. He most likely had never seen the city of Jerusalem for

> Nehemiah stepped into the pages of history when he decided to stand up and do something about the Broken Places of his people and their beloved city Jerusalem.

himself. But there was one thing Nehemiah had cultivated: he had favor with the king of Persia.

History changes because people, normal everyday people like you and I, find our part to play in it—each one of us playing a vital, urgent part towards the whole.

As a musician, I am immediately drawn to the reality of an orchestra, with dozens of instruments. What hope does the quiet flute have of being heard when placed next to the blaring trumpets? But at just the right moment, just the right time, each instrument, both "great" and "small," is called to the forefront to play its part in producing the beauty and completeness of the whole. Each instrument is not heard with the same volume or loudness, nor does each one play for the same amount of time in the musical piece... but who among us would ever want to hear an orchestra of only tubas? Each musical contribution is needed to produce the orchestral sound.

As the Bible records for us, Nehemiah stepped into the pages of history when he decided to stand up and do something about the Broken Places of his people and their beloved city Jerusalem. He didn't allow the doubts and fears that most certainly plagued his mind to have the opportunity or authority to rule his heart.

Nehemiah, the one destined to bring God's comfort to His broken people (see Isaiah 40:1), was about to become a Restorer and Rebuilder.

In this, the book of Nehemiah strongly resembles Exodus and the Broken Place the Israelites were in after 210 years of slavery, when Moses stepped forward to rebuild his broken people. Nehemiah and Moses were both put in places by God that were somewhat disconnected from the brokenness of the people. While the nation in both periods of history was struggling physically and spiritually, both Nehemiah and Moses had their place in the palace of the king. Yet they both chose not to remain there, but instead to fulfill their divinely assigned role to serve their people and lead them to a better place.

An unlikely hero would again rise from among the people of Israel and help to usher in a new era to heal their broken past.

Be careful as you read these next pages… because Nehemiah's Hope and commitment are infectious. You may find yourself stirred to look with fresh eyes at the Broken Places in and around your life, and you may just find yourself part of Nehemiah's story.

FOR FURTHER STUDY:

1. What portion or portions of the biblical story of Israel resemble your story of your own journey with God? How so?

_____

_____

_____

_____

_____

2. In what areas of your life have you struggled the most to trust the goodness of God?

_____

_____

_____

_____

_____

_____

_____

3. What doubts or fears do you have that are keeping you from rebuilding Broken Places in your life? How can you begin to face them?

_____

_____

_____

_____

_____

4. Reflect on the statement, "Hope is Remembering things which are Yet to Be." What would true Hope look like in a situation you are facing right now?

_____

_____

_____

_____

_____

_____

CHAPTER 2

THE REPORT AND THE RESPONSE

STIRRING YOURSELF TO ACTION

"To build a future, you have to know the past."

—Otto Frank, German businessman
and Holocaust survivor[5]

Favor.

What is it? *WHY* is it?

Why is it that you can take certain people and put them into almost any circumstance, and they seem to rise to the top? They seem to stand out?

Luck? Chance?

I don't think so. I think "favor" (or "charisma" or whatever you want to call it) is the result of a long-term commitment to certain

Nehemiah was living in the city of Susa, the same city Esther had lived in not long before him.

core beliefs and disciplines that prepare you to maximize the moments that present themselves to you in life.

I have taught my sons, over and over (they can recite it by heart):

"What is needed for success in life is...

- A strong faith in the God of the Bible
- A strong work ethic
- Excellent manners."

Whatever favor is, Nehemiah certainly had it. He became the cupbearer of the king in the palace at Susa—an esteemed position, a trusted position of a counselor, wise friend, and associate of the king. He was in an exalted position, even though he was in exile. He was a slave, but he was living in luxury, with every need met. Besides doing his job, he had really only one priority: don't cause any trouble for the king.

Nehemiah was living in the city of Susa, the same city Esther had lived in not long before him. Because of Esther's courage, the people of Israel were preserved from the evil plot of Haman, and her courage was commemorated as Purim, a national feast holiday for the Jews, after they were saved from annihilation.

Nehemiah would have known the details of Esther's story and likely was inspired by her courage and strategy. But to be saved from extermination, as dramatic as the breakthrough had been in Esther's day, was just the first step of God's plan. Israel was alive, but still in exile. She was not Home.

> **We cannot make Survival our Home. It does not have the ability to sustain us for a life worth living.**

SURVIVAL VS. SACRIFICE

Sometimes we can learn more from what is *not* written, than what *is* written. The book of Esther finishes on a great high for the Jews of Persia. Esther and her uncle Mordecai saved the day for the Jews of Persia, but that was where it ended. There was no great awakening of the Jews showing that Exile was not the place for them and that Israel was their homeland. In fact, the book of Ezra details that only 42,360 returned at that time.

Many of us, sadly, face seasons in which our life is not about victory or fulfillment. It is just about survival. We find ourselves not able to even think about true, long-term abundance. Instead, we are literally wondering—will my marriage survive? Will my family survive? Will my business, my church survive?

Trauma marks the soul. Those of us who have survived multiple forms of abuse, sometimes from multiple abusers, are tasked with the long journey of moving towards healing and freedom. But survival is our first priority—*sometimes, literal physical survival.*

Esther's story was the story of the survival of the Jews. Survival is necessary. But survival is only a step, if we are still in exile—if

> **The promise of Hope calls us to truly return Home, albeit with great cost and sacrifice.**

we still are not Home. In other words, we cannot make Survival our Home. It does not have the ability to sustain us for a life worth living, even in apparent opulence.

In Esther's day, the Jews were sitting very comfortably at the table of the Persian king Ahasuerus, which would explain Esther's initial reluctance to act on behalf of her people. There are even rabbinical commentaries that believe the vessels that were used at the king's banquet were vessels stolen from the Temple itself, yet many of the Jews sat there in the palace indulging in the comforts offered to them. It was a false happiness, an affluent but empty survival.

Many times, we build for ourselves impressive structures in our land of captivity, and we pretend that they have taken the place of Home. We try to project happiness and fulfillment and try to convince ourselves that we should be content to "settle" for the good things we have, even though the promise of Hope is still calling us to truly return Home, albeit with great cost and sacrifice.

This is true of the Jewish people who throughout the generations became like Nehemiah, prominent members of society, respected and influential in many countries around the world. They built homes, businesses, Jewish schools, ritual baths, and everything a Jew needs to survive. Yet three times a day, even now, a Jew turns towards Jerusalem from wherever he or she is and prays for its rebuilding. For 2,000 years of exile, even when they have been comfortable in that exile, the Jews have maintained the national focus on their homeland and on Jerusalem.

In Persia, a new era was appearing to the people of Judah on the near horizon. It was time to go Home. To Restore and Rebuild. But in order for that to manifest, it required someone to rise and take action.

Here is where Nehemiah is remarkable. Remember, Nehemiah was serving in the household of the wealthiest ruler on the planet. Every need that he had was attended to… every comfort that he possibly could have had was cared for as a servant of the king. Contrary to what would be expected for a people in captivity, he was living in opulence and splendor. This wasn't Wal-Mart… it was Neiman Marcus! Nehemiah's position was a coveted place of influence and favor. The last thing he should have done was rock the boat.

NEHEMIAH'S RESPONSE

And then, Nehemiah receives a visit from his long-lost brother and some of his friends.

> …Hanani one of my brethren came with men from Judah; and I asked them concerning the Jews who had escaped, who had survived the captivity, and concerning Jerusalem. And they said to me, "The survivors who are left from the captivity in the province are there in great distress and reproach. The

wall of Jerusalem is also broken down, and its gates are burned with fire" (Nehemiah 1:2-3).

Nehemiah learns that all the things that should have marked their blessing, their "chosen-ness" before God, were lying in ruins in their Home. All the things that should have been speaking of the special relationship that God had with the children of Israel were at that moment lying in destruction. Instead of being a visible testimony of the faithfulness of God and His blessing on the people of God, Israel seemed to now have a "testimony" of destruction, abandonment, and sadness. The rubble of Jerusalem silently mocked the promises of God.

And then we see what for me is one of the most absolutely amazing moments in history—certainly the most amazing part of this story. Nehemiah receives this report, and what is his response?

So it was, when I heard these words, that I sat down and wept, and mourned for many days; I was fasting and praying before the God of heaven (v. 4).

Why?

I have asked myself this question literally dozens of times, maybe a hundred times or more.

WHY, when Nehemiah received this report, did it move him so profoundly, so deeply, that he wept and fasted and prayed?

2. THE REPORT AND THE RESPONSE

What is it and why is it that some people are MOVED to great action, response, courage, and sacrifice when presented with certain realities, and others just shuffle off to a safe distance with mutterings of "That's sad…" and by their silence, saying, "I cannot, will not, get involved."

Nehemiah had every reason to leave well enough alone. To do nothing; say nothing. To take whatever his feelings may have been, minimize them, hide them, and thus blunt them. To make his heart hard. To avoid tears. TO NOT CARE. He had every reason to do what so many of us do day after day after day—which is *nothing*. It made far more sense for him to mumble some sentimental words of "Oh, that is such a shame… sorry to hear that…" and be done with it.

That is what we do, what I do, far too often.

But there is something deep within Nehemiah—the deepest place of his being—which causes him anguish that will ultimately lead to action. He weeps, he fasts, and he prays (as we all should and must do), but then he commits himself to action. Life-altering, no-turning-back, all-in, come-hell-or-high-water action.

Nehemiah became laser-focused in his soul, and in his spirit, on what was happening. Because he believed in the Word of God, he believed in the way things *should* be. And the way things *should be* and the way things *were* at that moment were radically different— so someone needed to come and stand in the gap.

THE CHARACTER OF A RESTORER

The prerequisite for Nehemiah in that moment was that he cared. The heart of God and the Word of God were in him, and it made all the difference. Nehemiah cared more about the reputation of the Lord than about his own comfort. He cared more about the Kingdom of God coming forth than living personally in a mode of complacent ease.

Nehemiah was moved to action.

So, be careful. Because if you continue reading, YOU may be stirred to action. You may be required to move from Survival to Return. The Spirit of God, as never before, is looking in this generation for Restorers and Repairers. He is looking for those with a Nehemiah heart. He is looking for those who will weep, fast, pray, and then courageously act.

We are living in an hour today when, more than ever, we need to move out of the place of religious "merry-go-round" Christian life into the place of confronting culture with authority and relevance and the word of the Lord, with lifestyles to back up our words. If there ever was a time when this is needed, it is today. We are in that place right now.

When Nehemiah got the report, he not only physically received it, but he also took it with him into an extended time of fasting and prayer. Nehemiah's response was that he *acted* on the report. As is discussed in the Talmud, "Great is the learning that brings one to action."

What was it about Nehemiah's character to not be content in the lap of luxury?

Instead of giving way to complacency, his actions declared, "In the place between what *is* and what *should be* (a gap), I've got to get involved and make a difference, *because the name and character of my God is at stake.*"

Though he was living in a foreign land, Nehemiah never lost his close connection to the name of God over His people and over His land. For Nehemiah, Jerusalem was the city where God had placed His very name (2 Chronicles 6:6). What was at stake with those broken-down walls was the fame, the very reputation of God. Stirred to see the awareness of God's name restored in his generation, Nehemiah stood up and committed himself to getting involved.

DID YOU KNOW?

Royalty and Captivity: King Artaxerxes I, whom Nehemiah served in the court at Susa, was the son of Xerxes I (Ahasuerus), by whom Esther was appointed Queen, also in Susa.

AUDIENCE WITH THE KING AND THE KING

So in chapter 2, Nehemiah begins his action plan by going to the king on behalf of his land and his people.

37

> **In our journey from Exile to Home, we will have to take never-turning-back steps. They will demand great courage.**

Why?

Because God is a God of order, of process, and of strategy. Nehemiah had proven himself a faithful, loyal, trustworthy servant. And now was the moment to take all his accumulated favor, what Stephen Covey calls the "emotional bank account," and make a pretty massive withdrawal.

But before Nehemiah meets with his earthly king, he meets with his heavenly King. For this must always be our pattern.

Trust in the Lord with all your heart, and lean not on your own understanding; in all your ways acknowledge Him, and He shall direct your paths (Proverbs 3:5-6).

Having sought God earnestly in prayer, coming in repentance on behalf of his people's sin of turning away from the Lord, Nehemiah knows that his next step is to seek the favor of the kingly authority. The conclusion of Nehemiah's prayer in chapter 1 shows him at this crossroads:

"O Lord, I pray, please let Your ear be attentive to the prayer of Your servant, and to the prayer of Your servants who desire to fear Your name; and let Your servant prosper this day, I pray, and grant him mercy in the sight of this man." For I was the king's cupbearer (v. 11).

Nehemiah had to face his own fears in taking this never-turn-back step.

In our journey from Exile to Home, we will have to take never-turn-back steps. They demand great courage. Courage is something we hear less and less about these days. Courage is only for the movies today, it seems—not something we need in everyday life. But of course, it is needed now more than ever.

In his fateful moment, Nehemiah took the wine to serve the king, as he did every day. The king noticed his downcast countenance, which he had never seen before in his cupbearer. When the king questioned him, Nehemiah's account says that he became "dreadfully afraid" (2:2). Then, risking his own standing and probably his life before this powerful ruler, he launched out into the deep by declaring his seemingly impossible and unreasonable request:

"May the king live forever! Why should my face not be sad, when the city, the place of my fathers' tombs, lies waste, and its gates are burned with fire?"

Then the king said to me, "What do you request?"
So I prayed to the God of heaven. And I said to the king, "If it pleases the king, and if your servant has found favor in your sight, I ask that you send me to Judah, to the city of my fathers' tombs, that I may rebuild it" (vv. 3-5).

> **Nehemiah was almost certainly giving up his rare position. But God had gone before him.**

Notice, even while speaking with the king, Nehemiah was inwardly interceding. Nehemiah knew that he was putting it all on the line for the sake of his God and his homeland. He gives us the powerful example of action and intercession as completely and continuously combined, not separated.

It feels to me that much of the Western Church seems to fall into two camps. We have the "intercession" and "prophetic" camp that emphasizes sacred assemblies, day and night prayer, and prophetic gatherings. And we have the "activist" camp that emphasizes legislation, public policy, and voting. It seems to me that we need to take a lesson from Nehemiah. Prayer and action should be consistently walked out together, one naturally leading into the other as we recognize that the Holy Spirit is leading and guiding us.

Nehemiah's position as trusted confidant required him to be available to the king on a constant basis. In asking to travel to Jerusalem, Nehemiah was almost certainly giving up his rare position and could quite possibly be viewed as betraying the king's trust, which could have angered the king and resulted in Nehemiah's imprisonment or even worse.

But God had gone before him.

The king (and queen, the Bible says in 2:6) began to ask him what he needed and how they could help. Nehemiah realized that a *kairos* moment had come... a moment of rare, divine favor that must be seized and walked through.

And so, with the favor that was flowing, he asked for and received largely from the king. He received letters of endorsement, letters of financial assistance, and essentially the full backing and authority of the king. This became so important in just a few chapters, when enemies rose up to attempt to stop his progress.

What if Nehemiah had not lived a life that earned favor with the king? What if, upon receiving the report from his brothers, he made an emotional decision and left in the dead of night to try to accomplish this on his own? What if he decided that the "burden on his heart" was more important than the protocols and process of government and right order? He might have even called that the "leading of the Holy Spirit," as so many of us do when pulled by our own emotions, unwilling to wait and walk in wisdom.

If he had tried this on his own strength, he certainly would have failed. But he lived and worked within a mindset that understood that even though he was serving a king who did not recognize his God, that God certainly was still ruling over all.

And now, having walked in passion, prayer, courage, and wisdom, Nehemiah was ready for this epic journey. Let's journey with him.

FOR FURTHER STUDY:

1. Are you usually slow or quick to step out in a new idea or project? What are a few ways you could use this tendency as a strength and not a weakness?

_____

_____

_____

_____

_____

_____

2. Would you say you are "surviving" or "thriving" in your life currently? Why?

_____

_____

_____

_____

_____

3. Choose one aspect of Nehemiah's response in this part of the story that you want to emulate. Explain.

_____

_____

_____

_____

_____

_____

4. What is one beginning action that you can take TODAY to step out in what God has already spoken to you about?

_____

_____

_____

_____

_____

_____

_____

Chapter 3

THE JOURNEY HOME

FINDING YOUR COURAGE IN THE RUBBLE

"The summit of happiness is reached when a person is ready to be what he is."

—Erasmus
16th-century Dutch theologian[6]

9**00 miles.**

That was the distance from Susa to Jerusalem. From Exile to Home. Or what used to be Home, but was now a mockery of what once was.

900 miles.

It is so hard for us to conceive, in today's "hop on a plane" world, what long-distance travel would have meant in history up until a couple hundred years ago.

> **The journey from Exile to Home is always long, arduous, and fraught with peril.**

Weather, the need for food and water, caring for your travel animals, the fear of bandits, the fear of wild animals, the fear of getting lost... ample opportunities for every trip to be your last.

But there was a passion that lived inside of Nehemiah, which I am believing lives inside you as well. This passion caused Nehemiah to WEEP and ANGUISH over the report from his brothers; it FUELED him as he began this most epic, life-threatening, life-defining journey.

The journey from Exile to Home, the journey to Restore and Rebuild, is always long. It is always arduous. It is always fraught with peril. Our 900 miles is probably not geographic, but there may be 900 miles of all sorts of adventure awaiting us once we commit ourselves to a life of Journey, a life of Returning Home.

Everyone is the strongest critic of things he or she was raised in, so forgive me in advance. But one of my strongest concerns regarding modern Western Christianity is its focus on *events* in our spiritual life, rather than *journey* of our spiritual life. Specifically, we talk about "getting saved," then some portions of the Church talk about "getting filled with the Spirit," then we talk about "receiving an anointing" or "walking in revival."

We subconsciously, I think, set ourselves up for a mindset of going from spiritual high to spiritual high.

> **A true commitment to a life of spiritual depth is a commitment to the Journey.**

But as far as I can see, a true commitment to a life of spiritual depth is a commitment to the Journey from Exile to Home, a Journey that is often dangerous, often lonely, often difficult, but oh-so-worth-it.

When we present a "quick fix" Christianity, we ultimately set people up for disappointment. When we invite them to an epic spiritual Journey, we are being more honest and preparing them for a life of true faith.

In the Temple, there were many sacrifices brought on special occasions, whether it was to celebrate a significant event in one's life, the occasion of a Festival, or the need to bring an offering as part of spiritual healing from sin. However, the most important sacrifice was the Korban Tamid, the "consistent sacrifice" (Exodus 29:38-42). It was sacrificed once in the morning and once in the evening. No matter the day, no matter the occasion, it was consistent. Consistency on the journey is a lot *more boring* and *less exciting* than the special occasions, the highlights. But with consistency of the day-in, day-out service of God—often through strains and difficulties—the highs are much higher and more impactful.

Who knows what difficulties Nehemiah faced on this 900-mile journey? Scripture does not say. But we do know a few things: it was hot. Relentlessly hot. His camels stunk. They had to constantly ration and be concerned for water and food. They had to constantly be on the lookout for bandits. In other words, even if his Journey went exceptionally well, with little trouble, it was still a far cry from the ease and opulence of the palace.

Spiritual Journey, the Return Home, requires great sacrifice, every time.

STANDING IN THE GATES

After a few months, Nehemiah finally arrived in Jerusalem (Nehemiah 2:11).

Can you imagine his emotions? I would guess it was a mixture of great excitement and great despair. He was seeing, for the first time, the land of his Promise.

But... it was devastated and in ruins.

But... at least he was THERE.

He was finally assessing REALITY, not just dreaming about it.

As Nehemiah prepared to take his first actual look around his mission on the ground, he already had opposition beginning to line up against him. Scripture says there were neighboring enemies who were "deeply disturbed that a man had come to seek the well-being of the children of Israel" (v. 10).

First, Nehemiah led a secretive scouting party. They rode out in the middle of the night to go look over Jerusalem under cover of darkness. (Why hasn't Hollywood told this

> **"Normal" is one of the first and greatest sacrifices on the altar of calling.**

story?) He and his team were in danger because the walls were broken down, and there were vandals as well as those who had vowed their opposition to the project; but Nehemiah and his men were determined to scout out the territory.

Gone were the palace, the comfort, the luxurious foods and the servants at Nehemiah's command. "Normal" was GONE.

"Normal" is one of the first and greatest sacrifices on the altar of calling.

Now, all of a sudden, it was the heat of the desert and the discomforts and dangers of traveling that had become Nehemiah's daily realities. Water itself became a luxury as they spied out the land that had been broken down.

So there was Nehemiah, surveying the situation and developing a plan—with no guarantees of success but with a sense in his heart that he was in the beginning stages of a divine mission. After secretly scouting out Jerusalem, Nehemiah met with the local leaders that had remained in Judah and cast his vision before them:

> *Then I said to them, "You see the distress that we are in, how Jerusalem lies waste, and its gates are burned with fire.*

> **God is looking to knit together hearts, lives, and destinies. Find your tribe!**

Come and let us build the wall of Jerusalem, that we may no longer be a reproach." And I told them of the hand of my God which had been good upon me, and also of the king's words that he had spoken to me.

So they said, "Let us rise up and build." Then they set their hands to this good work (2:17-18).

Here lies an important step in Restoring and Rebuilding. Find those of like heart and join together. They have been waiting for you. You see, God uses individuals, but there are no superstars. There are no Lone Rangers. In fact, the truest test of a genuine leader is the strength and longevity of the team around him. God is looking to knit together hearts, lives, and destinies. Find your tribe! Find a group of like-hearted world-changers and do the hard work of developing authentic relationships as the fulcrum for historic change.

DEVASTATION IN THE RUBBLE

Yad Vashem.

The Holocaust Memorial in Jerusalem.

Every time I take Christian pilgrims to Israel, the horrific, nightmarish images that confront us at Yad Vashem beat mercilessly into our consciousness, a surreal yet undeniable reminder of the atrocities of which human hatred is capable. But as profoundly unnerving as it is for Christians to be exposed to these historic accounts, it can only begin to describe the horror and devastation that *Jewish* people encounter when they see (and in seeing, relive) the genocidal hatred that their own parents and grandparents suffered through.

There is something exceptionally confrontational and jarring about going to the center of your own pain and facing the deepest questions that you find there.

That is why we are so good at forming all kinds of patterns of avoidance and distraction, which become *lifestyles* of avoidance and distraction.

Although Nehemiah's company had heard the sad reports from Judah, nothing could have fully prepared them for what they faced when they actually saw the devastation of their Home. Before they could make plans for a physical rebuilding project, they had to face the reality of the pain that their people had experienced.

Though it was a collective experience of loss for the Israelites, it was also an intensely personal one. Each man and woman had to face his or her own fears in order to move forward in the next chapter of God's plan for them as a people.

After arriving in Jerusalem, Nehemiah and his company had to squarely confront the tough, unanswered, existential questions... *Why did God allow this to happen? Has He forgotten us? Won't*

> **God is extending the opportunity to find your true identity, in the rubble of broken dreams and broken-down walls.**

this project fail even if we do find a way to begin? What will happen to our families if it does fail?

How did they find the resolve, the energy to press on? I believe that at the deepest level, they knew that unless this piece of who they really were was resurrected from that dust and rubble, they would continue to be an incomplete, hollow version of their true selves, both individually and as a people. And the pain of that thought was enough to push them past obstacles to begin the hard and daunting work.

Today in whatever challenge you find yourself, I believe God is extending the opportunity to find your true self, your true identity, in the rubble of broken dreams and broken-down walls—to find courage again in terrible circumstances where there never could be courage, except for the presence of the God who gives us courage and calling to rebuild Broken Places.

The story of Nehemiah shows us that in order to rebuild Broken Places in our lives, each of us in a very real way has to journey Home again.

COME INTO THE HOUSE OF GOD

Modern pop psychology is full of an emphasis on self-maintenance and self-care, based on the premise that we can do anything that we set our minds to. We can hire a personal fitness trainer, we can research and implement the "perfect diet" for our bodies, we can set effective boundaries in relationships, we can achieve our career goals through strategic self-branding, and on and on. At the center of this thinking is the belief that if you can think it, you can be it—and that the results lie within your ability to train yourself to learn the right skills so that you can achieve what you desire.

There is certainly truth to the principle that the way we think determines the quality of our life. The Bible itself supports it! Proverbs 23:7 says, "For as [a man] thinks in his heart, so is he." Proverbs 21:5 adds regarding thoughtful diligence, "The plans of the diligent lead surely to plenty, but those of everyone who is hasty, surely to poverty."

However, if we take this by itself without the balance of other truths God has put in place (such as Jeremiah 17:9, "The heart is deceitful above all things, and desperately wicked; who can know it?"), we don't have the complete picture. If we are honest, we will recognize that we have significant limitations in our knowledge of what is best for our lives. We may take a calculated business risk only to see it go down in flames; we may monitor our diet fastidiously and still encounter personal health crises that are out of our control; we may read extensively on how to achieve healthy relationships and still come upon relational brokenness even in our immediate family.

> **"Home" is the community and surroundings in which we uncover our true identity.**

When we make our worst mistakes, when we walk through the darkest unexpected valleys, or when we experience the most terrible Broken Places in our lives, there is a hard-wiring within us that seeks out covenantal relationships and our true *Home*. To journey Home again is to return to the place of healing, the place of truth, and the place of solid counsel and bedrock-level foundations.

"Home" is a physical place but is also a greater defining reality: it is the community and surroundings in which we uncover our true identity. For Nehemiah and his company, it was both these things — a physical city (Jerusalem) and a community (the Jews) who found their Jewish identity in relationship with God and each other.

My life and ministry work have taken me to a wide plethora of places over the years, near and far. No matter where I go, when the joys and challenges of life on the road give way to a coming home once again, it is a welcome sight for this weary traveler.

Several years ago, when coming home to Buffalo, New York, after an extended trip, my oldest son Isaac was there at the airport arrivals area with his guitar with an unexpected gift and greeting for me. He launched into a personalized song that he had written to show his appreciation for me as a father and for our special relationship through the years.

What a way to come home! I was blown away and it was an amazing surprise, and especially meaningful coming from my own son who has been with me through the highs and lows of the last 20 years of my life in ministry. For me it signified, after a long and difficult trip, a returning back to the place where the deepest relationships are—those that will matter forever—and recalibrating to that identity again, brushing off the dust from the long journey.

In order to rebuild what once was, each of us must go to the source and foundation on which our life was built, which ultimately is God Himself. For those who believe in God, our true Home is the house of God—not merely a physical building but a spiritual place of relational intimacy where His words define and heal us, the place that is at the core of who He is and who we are before Him.

In Exodus 25:8, God commands, "Make Me a sanctuary [Tabernacle], that I may dwell among [or within] them." This can be a confusing statement. If the Jews made a Tabernacle, was God intending to dwell within IT or THEM? The Rabbis teach that here God is referring to the physical Tabernacle as well as the spiritual one inside all of us. If we build for Him a Tabernacle, a Holy of Holies, He will dwell within us. Not only is God's Home our Home, but we also are actually a home, a resting place for God.

Many of us would rather not go there. To return Home is to navigate through overgrown areas that have become snares and entanglements through years of neglect. It is not pleasant to face one's own brokenness. In the short term at least, it would be much easier to try to forget the past, pretend it never happened, and start again. But eventually if we don't face our inward pain, it can resurface in even more disruptive ways in the future and threaten to completely derail us. Like an adopted person meeting his or her biological parents for the first time, each of us has received from God a desire to know where we come from and to know the truth that has formed us. To return to the place where our brokenness began is the only true way to rebuild on a solid foundation.

Jesus invited us with Him into *His* Father's house when He said,

Come to Me, all you who labor and are heavy laden, and I will give you rest. Take My yoke upon you and learn from Me, for I am gentle and lowly in heart, and you will find rest for your souls (Matthew 11:28-29).

To return Home is not easy. It will require deep questions and heartfelt courage. But Home is the place where we will gain clarity and find our true identity in the midst of the rubble of broken dreams and the ashes of disappointment.

DID YOU KNOW?

Susa Today: Susa, the site of the Persian palace, is located at the town of Shush in the western portion of modern-day Iran, near the Iraq border and the Iraqi southern city of Basra. Susa is also the traditional site of the tomb of Daniel.

FOR FURTHER STUDY:

1. Is the idea of "Home" a naturally safe place for you? Why or why not?

_____

_____

_____

_____

_____

_____

_____

2. Define the word *journey* in your own words. Does this inspire fear or excitement when you think about it? (Or another emotion?)

_____

_____

_____

_____

_____

_____

3. What is one practical way that the Jewish people have been able to survive the pain and devastation of their past? How could this approach apply to your life?

_____

_____

_____

_____

_____

4. Read Matthew 11:28-29. What do these words of Jesus mean to your own journey of faith?

_____

_____

_____

_____

_____

5. What is one aspect of your identity that you want to grow in?

_____

_____

CHAPTER 4

BECOMING A WALL BUILDER

WHICH WALLS ARE YOU BUILDING?

"Everything can be taken from a man but one thing: the last of the human freedoms—to choose one's attitude in any given set of circumstances, to choose one's own way."

–Viktor Frankl
Austrian philosopher and Holocaust survivor[7]

Walls.

What picture or emotion does this word bring to your heart? Is your first response positive or negative? Or mixed?

Many times, we conceive of walls negatively. For example, what parent has not said to a teenager, "I feel like there is a wall between us when we talk!"?

Within the church world and society at large, we often speak of walls of division, walls of misunderstanding, ignorance, racism, and denominationalism.

> **There are some walls that are good and right and helpful—the type of walls that we *want* in our society.**

These are walls that separate, walls that divide, walls that weaken. They weaken us because they fracture and separate the body of Christ, or society as a whole, from mutual cooperation. We even refer to walls as something to break out of, to "get outside the four walls of the church," so that we can go and make an impact in the world around us.

But deeper consideration tells us that there are also some walls that are good and right and helpful—the type of walls that we *want* in our society. As believers, our view is that God wants to build these in our generation. These are walls of righteousness and justice, walls of peace and security, and walls that serve as a hedge of protection around individuals and families so that the enemy cannot break through.

Sometimes it can be difficult to determine what kind of wall a particular wall is. In the Jewish community, it is customary for a marriage ceremony to take place under a *chuppah*. At that time, the bride circles the groom seven times. There are two interpretations to this. Some say that she is re-enacting Jericho and breaking down the walls between them. The other opinion is exactly the opposite—that she is building a protective wall around her husband and promising to guard him from that which could harm him and their relationship.

So we must understand—we must discern—which walls should be built and which walls should be torn down. For example, in difficult times, family members walking through stress with one another may need to put in place "healthy boundaries" (another

Much of life is about knowing and discerning when to build walls and when to tear them down.

name for a type of wall), but then, hopefully later, also know the time to let those boundaries relax, so that in vulnerability, healing and growth can occur.

Much of life is about knowing and discerning when to build walls and when to tear them down.

Nehemiah had discerned the situation in his generation. Good walls, necessary walls, historic walls, covenantal walls, had broken down.

It was time to rebuild them.

WALLS TO TEAR DOWN

The prophet Jeremiah, whose prophecy framed the 70 years that the people of Israel would be held in captivity, embodied the tearing down of unrighteous walls to prepare God's people to rebuild once again on solid foundations.

Jeremiah's calling from the Lord was a true prophetic call:

> **Jeremiah's first assignment from the Lord (as is often the case with God's prophets) was to tear down and root out systems of thinking that were not honoring to God.**

Then the Lord put forth His hand and touched my mouth, and the Lord said to me:

"Behold, I have put My words in your mouth.

See, I have this day set you over the nations and over the kingdoms,

To root out and to pull down,

To destroy and to throw down,

To build and to plant" (Jeremiah 1:9-10).

Jeremiah's first assignment from the Lord (as is often the case with God's prophets) was to tear down and root out systems of thinking that were not honoring to God. As the people of Judah moved farther down a road of rebellion against God, Jeremiah pleaded with the people to repent and turn back, but his messages fell on mostly deaf ears.

Prophets, in the truest sense, are not necessarily those who may predict the future, but rather, those who discern and then confront wrong, ungodly patterns of thinking and behavior and call us higher. As was the case with Jeremiah, those who are called by the Lord to be prophets can often be seen in a negative light by the people. In fact, Jeremiah was thrown in prison by the very Jews he was trying to reach in Judah.

The prophets confronted in the people of God those ungodly walls that they were building (knowingly or not) by their sinful choices.

> **The building of ungodly walls, when allowed to develop, brings harmful and divisive outcomes that result in hopelessness and brokenness.**

Today, just as we see in the story of Israel and Judah, the building of these ungodly walls, when allowed to develop, brings harmful and divisive outcomes that result in hopelessness and brokenness. What are some of the unrighteous walls that we see in our own generation?

WALLS OF OFFENSE

Every day, we have opportunities to be offended. And increasingly, we seem to be living in a culture where everyone is offended, with everything, all the time.

Inevitably, something happens with someone in our life—maybe a member of our family or a member of our church. Perhaps a small incident, a comment, a look that we don't like.

And internally, without telling anyone else, we "make a note" of it. In other words, we give attention to what happened, and assign, if not blame, at least possible doubt about the other person's motives. The Bible calls this "keeping a record of wrong."

And this little thing—a comment, a glance, a small action—becomes a brick, a stone. We may lay it down and not actively hold it, but it is there; and the next time something happens with that individual, another brick, another stone, is laid in place. Sometimes slowly, sometimes quickly, a wall, a mindset, a judgment, comes into place.

All of us are subject to having negative experiences that we can easily perceive as an unjust attack. Without submitting to the Holy Spirit to order our thoughts, we very quickly can be put off by the comment of another or deeply hurt by someone, including—and sometimes even especially—our leaders.

Unchecked, undealt with, small offenses quickly become walls of self-protection if we aren't careful. Our closest relationships can suddenly become our enemy when bitterness and offense set in. Placing one small stone on top of another, one small offense on top of another small offense, we soon have erected a fortified wall to keep others out.

Our disappointments in life, when we turn them into actions of judging others or assigning blame onto others, can become "dis-appointments" by which we miss the appointed assignments that God has for us to bring us blessing.

WALLS OF DIVISION

In much of the Western Church today, we have lost the concept that is intuitive to the Jewish world: the idea of our corporate identity, our mystical and yet very real covenantal community.

One of my dear Jewish friends, after spending a couple years getting to know many in the evangelical community, said something to me one day that highlighted this very issue. From a sincere place of simply offering his perspective, he commented, "The thing I don't understand about you evangelical Christians is this—you don't seem to see yourselves as a unified people."

His comment stopped me dead in my tracks, and I realized that he had hit the nail on the head.

It reminded me of the words attributed by many to Saint Augustine, which could produce wonderful results if we would really meditate on them and incorporate them proactively into our lives:

"In essentials, unity; in non-essentials, liberty; in all things, charity."[8]

Because we don't see ourselves as a "people," we don't realize that we are mystically and yet truly linked together as "the body of Christ"—and we don't treat division and disunity as the poisonous thing that it so very often is.

The Apostle Paul exhorted the Corinthian church on this very issue:

Now therefore, it is already an utter failure for you that you go to law against one another. Why do you not rather accept wrong?... Do you not know that your bodies are members of Christ (1 Corinthians 6:7,15)?

For as the body is one and has many members, but all the members of that one body, being many, are one body, so also is Christ... that there should be no schism in the body, but that the members should have the same care for one another. And if one member suffers, all the members suffer with it; or if one member is honored, all the members rejoice with it (1 Corinthians 12:12, 25-26).

Our commitment to a local body of believers is seen as voluntary, often shallow, and easily forsaken in favor of a "better" church or group, especially as soon as an offense takes root.

What is the result of this shallow commitment? Sadly, we have more churches in the West that have been birthed out of division and disunity than from the multiplication that comes from the Spirit of God. We have become petty rather than maturing in the things of God, which prevents us from moving forward as a unified force for God's Kingdom.

We are weak, because we are divided. We are divided because we have not torn down walls which should be dismantled, and instead have built walls which should not be. What are some of the other negative walls that we must mark for demolition?

WALLS OF MANIPULATION

Even more insidious in some ways than walls of division are walls of manipulation, by which some "believers," including sometimes "leaders," conduct themselves as wolves in sheep's clothing to knowingly deceive others. Because of the deceit involved, these types of walls appear very positive on the outside but are actually a trap designed to ensnare others, to control a situation or to bring about a certain outcome to suit one's own desires. Speaking as someone who comes from the charismatic/Pentecostal community, we can sometimes be especially at risk for manipulation from charlatans who promise "signs and wonders."

Those who engage in building these types of walls are willing to engage in destructive behavior for the purpose of self-promotion or for the sake of advancing their own agenda. Persuasive by nature but also dishonest, those who build these walls have a selfish goal in mind and are willing to sacrifice the well-being of others (and even of the whole community) in order to achieve it.

WALLS OF FEAR

Fear is very often the deeper root issue behind other kinds of walls that we build around ourselves. When we operate in fear, we attempt to protect ourselves from being hurt by others—and we are often driven by inner promises or vows that we have made to "never allow someone to hurt us again."

However, it is actually impossible for our attempted preventative measures to succeed, because in our natural human experience the greatest hurt we feel often comes through those with whom we have the closest relationship. As a result, a preventative mindset can end up keeping us bound indefinitely by fear. When that happens, we have a growing tendency to shy away from the very Kingdom relationships that have the potential to bring us life.

A New Mindset

In all these types of walls, God is looking for a shift in our mindset—an inner decision to operate in a different way. It is too easy to adopt a mindset of individualism and consumerism, which says that everything is all about "me." The Kingdom of God calls us to a different value system.

What was "in it" for Nehemiah? Seemingly, nothing! He stood to lose everything in this quest. But he gave himself to the task for the glory of God and for the promises God had made to His people.

The Kingdom perspective says that we are vessels of His glory and His honor, to release the power of God into the world around us. This informs every aspect of our lives, including the need to submit to imperfect leaders. I realize that the concept of spiritual authority and godly submission to spiritual leaders is something that is almost never discussed today. Nevertheless, it is a vitally important reality of scriptural, Kingdom life.

Nehemiah was anointed by the Lord for the task of rebuilding the walls. He exercised that gift of leadership as he began the work.

But almost immediately, people around him began to resist his leadership and spiritual authority and work against it.

When it comes to submission to spiritual authority, mere agreement does not become a true submission to God and our leaders until there is actually a disagreement or reason to submit. Only when something rubs you the wrong way do you actually have an opportunity to submit. The people had a test in front of them.

In the days of Nehemiah and now, God allows things to "rub us the wrong way" to reveal something within us that He is working on. It is part of our dying to self. If we die to ourselves the way God intends, there is resurrection power and new life on the other side of the difficulty. But if we die according to the enemy's plan, we sacrifice our calling for the sake of selfish desires.

Choose your death well—take up your cross and follow the Lord! Remember what Paul said: "It is no longer I who live, but Christ lives in me; and the life which I now live in the flesh I live by faith in the Son of God, who loved me and gave Himself for me" (Galatians 2:20). We must count ourselves dead to the things of this world that we might become ALIVE to Christ!

I pray that you never become "dis-appointed" from what God wants to do, but that you will have the discernment through the Holy Spirit to recognize where bitter roots may be growing within you, so that you can heed the prophetic call to uproot them through God's strength and to tear down any negative walls that you have built.

> **The building of walls speaks of an apostolic anointing that mobilizes the whole of God's people to walk regionally in the strength of His purpose.**

WALLS TO BUILD UP

Thankfully, God's work in our lives individually and among His people does not end with the tearing down of negative walls. He has great plans for our lives, which involve our learning how to be wall builders according to His design.

Prophets are gifted in speaking of what is to come, and the biblical prophets served the God of Israel whose plans are for *good* and not for harm (see Jeremiah 29:11). Because of this, their messages ultimately were an uplifting declaration of His love and covenantal promises towards His people, including a glorious regathering of what God would accomplish in the future. They prophesied of a time when God's righteous walls would be built once again.

The building of walls speaks of an apostolic anointing that mobilizes the whole of God's people to walk regionally in the strength of His purpose. In the Kingdom of God, unity is paramount, and the apostles assemble God's people into the proper formation so that the corporate assignment can advance. We see Nehemiah walking in this anointing, to organize the work of the Lord to achieve success as God defines it, which is the building of His house in the earth.

In the 1970's, Kotaku Wamura, long-time mayor of Fudai, Japan, insisted on building a controversial, drab, 50-foot-high concrete seawall to guard his town from the dangers of the Pacific Ocean.

The floodgate wall was so massive that it took 12 years to build, at the cost of what would be $30 million today.

Many people objected to his plan, calling it too costly and unnecessary, and complaining that the wall would obstruct their beautiful view of the ocean. But Mayor Wamura had experiential reasons for persevering through the objections of villagers and politicians who disputed the expensive project, because in 1933, he had personally witnessed a tsunami destroy his town. By the time he was mayor, he believed it was within his ability to prevent history from repeating itself in Fudai.

Nearly 40 years later, on March 11, 2011, history proved him right.

On that day, a deadly tsunami induced by the magnitude-9.0 Great Sendai Earthquake struck the coastal areas of northeastern Japan. Although there was widespread devastation in many of the areas hit by the disaster, the town of Fudai emerged virtually unscathed. Countless lives and homes were spared. Mayor Wamura had died in 1997 without seeing the life-saving result of his efforts, but his persistence had saved his town.[9]

God's house has different kinds of walls, all of which help to carry out His purposes in the world around us. Let's consider some of those walls that God has appointed us to be part of building in this hour.

WALLS OF RIGHTEOUSNESS

Psalm 89:14 says of the God of Israel, "Righteousness and justice are the foundation of Your throne." There are many things that God builds, but they are all built upon the foundation stones of righteousness.

Righteousness is the integrity and right-standing of God's character expressed toward, in, and through His people. Applied to us as His children, it refers to uprightness in our relationship with God and each other.

To build righteous walls signifies that you as God's servant employ godly wisdom and that you consciously and consistently fortify the place of God's principles in your life—in your family, in your church, in your business, and in your region. God's promise to those who build walls of righteousness is that "no good thing will He withhold from those who walk uprightly" (Psalm 84:11).

WALLS OF JUSTICE

As another of the foundation stones of the throne of God, justice speaks of fairness and equality in the governance of human relationships. Because it is based on the dignity of human life and our equal standing as human beings before Almighty God, justice brings safety and security to our lives through the honoring of each individual person and each group of people.

Deuteronomy 16:20 declares, "Justice, and only justice, you shall pursue, so that you may live and possess the land which the Lord your God is giving you" (NASB). Justice is achieved through an active commitment to compassion and to valuing each human being in the sight of God. Justice is a supreme strength to society, allowing it to function in proper order and proper authority. God loves justice because He loves the world! His desire is for everyone to have the opportunity to grow, prosper, and find fulfillment as part of His Kingdom of righteousness.

DID YOU KNOW?

Second Temple Team: Nehemiah as governor and Ezra as scribe were both leaders of the people of Judah during the period of the Second Temple. In fact, many scholars believe the biblical books of Ezra and Nehemiah were originally one united book, chronicling the story of the rebuilding of Jerusalem.

WALLS OF UNITY

For much of the history of the Church, the people of God have faltered in exemplifying the type of unity that ushers in the fullness of God's purposes and plans in the earth. The original fracturing away from our Jewish, Hebraic roots that we were grafted into, has led to a constant pattern of split after split, rather than a heart seeking to reconcile. Nonessential disputes, along with the lack of genuine commitment to apostolic leadership, means we have not preserved the unity of our faith.

But God has something better for us as His people. Psalm 133:1 says, "Behold, how *good* and how *pleasant* it is for brethren to dwell together in unity!" (Emphasis added). Through the power of relationship, we are called to prefer one another (Romans 12:10; Philippians 2:3-4) and to continually come together as one in the act of worshipping and glorifying God (Romans 15:5-6).

If we will build walls of unity, God promises to *command* His blessing upon us (Psalm 133:3). That reality should be a great motivator for us to get involved and build the Kingdom of God together as His people.

WALLS OF LOVE

Colossians 3:14 says, "But above all these things put on love, which is the bond of perfection." Without love, every positive activity that we do is merely a good intention which may or may not endure. But as 1 Corinthians 13:7 reminds us, love is not bound by circumstances; rather, love transcends all situations as it "bears all things, believes all things, hopes all things, endures all things."

Far from just a superficial sentimentality, love is expressed in the hard work of daily relationships and in the humility to recognize and deal with one's own faults. It is an unconditional commitment to others around you that leads you to work for their good first before your own interests.

God is love (1 John 4:8), and if we would be wall builders in His Kingdom, we must build according to His character which is entirely ALL love—through and through. Everything else will eventually fall into ruin.

RESPONSE IN THE BROKENNESS

We cannot afford to waste our energies building unrighteous walls of division and offense. Living in that place of constant anger and frustration is exhausting, unfulfilling, and empty. Think of what would have happened if Nehemiah gave in to the negativity around him? If he allowed his soul to be polluted by the toxicity of others?

No, Nehemiah guarded his heart.

You see, we can go through all the hard work of identifying what caused the godly things in our lives to become broken, and even tearing down ungodly walls that we have built; but if we don't guard our hearts, we could end up very quickly rebuilding *un*righteous walls once again without even realizing it.

You might be saying today, "God, I have been down this road before of delving into the brokenness of my past, and it didn't end well. It would have been better for me to just ignore it and move on."

But if you will take just one step of courage and respond to the Holy Spirit's urging upon your heart, I believe that He will meet you there and begin to bring you into a new season—both of a

> **We must rebuild courageous, fortified, historic walls that will welcome the presence of God in our communities... to *remain* there.**

release from the negativity of the past and also of a rebuilding of the walls of God's purpose for the future.

If we as the body of Christ decide to become "unoffendable," not allowing ourselves to entertain the kind of negativity that will take our hearts off track, we will be positioned to partner with God and usher in a new day in history. We must rebuild courageous, fortified, historic walls that will welcome the presence of God in our communities... to *remain* there and bring exponential Kingdom fruit.

So the question I ask you now is, which walls are you building?

As a prophetic voice, Jeremiah tore down unrighteous walls and spoke of the things to come. The work was far from over! As an apostolic leader, Nehemiah later stepped into the apostolic call to rebuild what should be, to organize and assemble the people to carry out their God-given mission, and to manifest the heavenly (supernatural) things into the earthly (natural) realm.

Nehemiah was used by God to provide governance over the work and over the newly rebuilt city, so that the godly walls that they were rebuilding together could endure for future generations. This must always be a focus in the building of godly walls; we must continually prioritize the passing on of righteous values—and the history of what God has done—to the next generation, so that they have every opportunity to arise as faithful servants of the Lord and continue the good work.

It is because of their continual prioritization of transmitting their biblical value system to the next generation that the Jewish people have been able to endure centuries of opposition, attempts of genocide, and even divisions from within.

A revealing point about the way Jews pray is their reliance on community. They need at least ten men of the community, or a *minyan,* to pray together in order to fulfill the complete prayer. In addition, so many of their prayers are not about individual success, but rather about the success of the nation and even the entire world. This is a brilliant way to cultivate community. It is more about *our* success corporately than *my* success individually. Mutual success is far more beneficial to all of us than just one of us.

The Jews' mutual commitment to a culture of the Word of God and to fortifying righteous walls they have built has enabled them to stand as a people. Will we arise to the same holy task?

To do so, we must each have the grace to receive healing from the past, we must have a God-inspired vision for the future, and we must keep our hands and feet firmly planted in diligence in the present. This is what Nehemiah, one of history's greatest wall builders, teaches us.

FOR FURTHER STUDY:

1. Name one specific example each of both a positive and a negative "wall" that you have built in your life. What effect did each wall have on you at that time?

_____

_____

_____

_____

_____

_____

_____

2. Of the four types of negative walls mentioned in this chapter, which is your greatest pitfall? Explain.

_____

_____

_____

_____

_____

3. Of the four types of positive walls mentioned, which is your greatest strength? Explain.

_____

_____

_____

_____

_____

4. Why is it so important to be "unoffendable" in order to fully partner with God?

_____

_____

_____

_____

_____

_____

_____

CHAPTER 5

THE NOT-SO-SECRET ENEMY: SANBALLAT

YOUR RESPONSE AS A WATCHMAN TO THE ONSLAUGHT OF THE ENEMY

"What does it profit, my brethren, if someone says he has faith but does not have works? Can faith save him?... Thus also faith by itself, if it does not have works, is dead."

—James 2:14,17

The minute you decide to change, to grow, to rebuild—I promise you—you will soon encounter a character named Sanballat.

Sanballat may come in the form of a family member, a "friend," a co-worker, or even just a negative voice in your own head, speaking from your own limiting beliefs; but Sanballat—the voice of negativity, doubt, and mockery—will always appear.

Let's see this unfold in Nehemiah's story.

BRAMBLE-BUSH ENTRANCE

As soon as Nehemiah and the officials in Judah decided to take on the project of rebuilding the walls, Sanballat the Horonite, a governor in the Samaria region under the authority of the Persian Empire, appeared as the leader of the opposition movement. At the outset of the building project, Sanballat arrived with his band of naysayers, Tobiah the Ammonite and Geshem the Arab. The scripture says that they laughed at Nehemiah's company and openly despised their intentions (Nehemiah 2:19). Interestingly, Sanballat's name means "bramble-bush" and "enemy in secret."

Sanballat and his henchmen (more about them in the next chapter) had influence in the region and saw the presence of the builders as a threat to their control over the people of that area. They enjoyed their unchallenged position as the ones in power and did not intend to give way to an Israelite resurgence.

In short—there will always be those who view your success as a threat.

These people are hyper-critical of anyone seeking to bring change, to break outside the box, or to make a difference. Their insecurity and jealousy become the fuel for their attack on you and your work. Many times, as in this case, one of the first attacks your enemy will use is the attack of accusation. Look at how Sanballat accuses Nehemiah.

But when Sanballat the Horonite, Tobiah the Ammonite official, and Geshem the Arab heard of it, they laughed at us and despised us, and said, "What is this thing that you are doing? Will you rebel against the king" (2:19)?

Rebel against the king?

Remember, Nehemiah had very consciously and carefully received the blessing of the king, as well as letters of endorsement from the king (see 2:7-8). So, his heart was exactly the OPPOSITE of what he was being accused of.

The Sanballat spirit will always accuse you of wrong motives.

It's one of the oldest forms of attack in the enemy's playbook.

Understand this clearly. The question is not IF you will face Sanballat, but WHEN. The voice of accusation, mockery, doubt, and troublemaking WILL show up—in one form or another—when you begin to do serious work and make serious changes. But, forewarned is forearmed, as the old saying goes. If you know the voice of Sanballat is coming, you can more easily identify it when you see and hear it, and deal with it effectively so it doesn't stop your progress.

PLAN FOR OPPOSITION

Nehemiah's response demonstrated the level of confidence that had grown within him, convincing him that he was exactly where God wanted him to be:

> **Nehemiah understood this principle: opposition is oftentimes CONFIRMATION that you are on the right track.**

So I answered them, and said to them, "The God of heaven Himself will prosper us; therefore we His servants will arise and build, but you have no heritage or right or memorial in Jerusalem" (Nehemiah 2:20).

Nehemiah understood this principle: opposition is oftentimes CONFIRMATION that you are on the right track.

So in chapter 3, undeterred by the early opposition of Sanballat, and determined to begin even in the face of adversity, Nehemiah and his countrymen rolled up their sleeves and got to work. In great detail, Nehemiah implemented the plan by which different captains began the repairs on different sections of the wall, rehanging the doors at the gates surrounding the city and reconstructing the sections in between. The logistical coordination was quite involved as they began this massive undertaking.

Why is this so important?

Because you can have all the good intentions in the world, but they won't succeed without a PLAN and a TEAM.

Nehemiah is moving here in one of the key principles of building, which is outlined for us in Habakkuk.

Write the vision

And make it plain on tablets,

That he may run who reads it.

For the vision is yet for an appointed time;

But at the end it will speak, and it will not lie.

Though it tarries, wait for it;

Because it will surely come,

It will not tarry (Habakkuk 2:2-3).

The principles in this short section of scripture are so important for you as you rebuild.

WRITE your vision. There is something incredibly powerful and focusing when you sit down and don't just "wish" or "dream" about things, but you begin to write them out. It is your first step towards manifesting that dream. So do it. Find what works for you—a journal, or on your phone, or on your computer—whatever is best for you. But sit down, and WRITE the vision.

Make it PLAIN. In other words—fill in the details! Make it very step-by-step, precise, and clear. Think it through. How exactly will you get from point A to point B to point C?

Identify your TEAM. "That he may run who reads it" (v. 2). In other words, others are going to be involved in the implementation of your vision. Who do you need in your life to see this come to pass? And, just as importantly, identify those who will not be able to take the journey with you because of their own limiting beliefs

> **Once it became evident that the project was moving forward in earnest, the first wave of serious intimidation tactics came forth from Nehemiah's enemies.**

and viewpoints. You want those who can run with the vision—not those who will slow it down.

WAIT for it. You have to have patience.

Perseverance.

Determination.

Constant daily evaluation. And hourly and sometimes minute-by-minute decisions to move you towards your goal.

RESPONSE TO INTIMIDATION

Once it became evident that the project was moving forward in earnest, the first wave of serious intimidation tactics came forth from Nehemiah's enemies.

Sanballat shifted. He started out with mocking and intimidation, but as that did not work, he became enraged. He unleashed his ridicule and mocking among his own people against Nehemiah's company, saying:

"What are these feeble Jews doing? Will they fortify themselves? Will they offer sacrifices? Will they complete it

in a day? Will they revive the stones from the heaps of rubbish—stones that are burned" (Nehemiah 4:2)?

Notice that Sanballat's words were, "What are those feeble Jews doing?" He made a verbal attack on the character and ability of the Jews doing the work. He sought to discredit them by belittling their strength and trying to undermine their efforts through mocking.

Understand this as you decide to become a wall builder: the first plan of the enemy is to mock the word of God over your life. It doesn't matter who you are—there will always be a Sanballat!

The minute you get a dream, the minute you get a word from God, the minute you get a leading from the Holy Spirit, the minute you get a fresh hope and vision for your future... there will always be a Sanballat to bring a negative report, trying to steal the seed of God's vision for your life.

Sanballat tries to speak discouragement to your excitement and snatch the word of the promise from God. His negative scripts are all too familiar for many of us, from our past shortcomings: "You're a failure... you'll never be able to do it... who do you think you are?"

However it comes, the spirit of Sanballat will always be present to try to bring negativity and doubt and death to the Word of God in your life. So prepare when you get involved in rebuilding the wall, for the Sanballat effect to come into place—so that you can rise above the enemy's report and adhere instead to what God says.

At this key moment in chapter 4, Nehemiah made a very important decision. In the formative stages of the project, he had to put aside thoughts of his weakness or inability or lack of qualifications.

Remember, Nehemiah was in this spot after he had left the palace, after he had left the comfort zone where he had become established, after he had left the beauty and opulence of the life that he was in. He had left it all because he realized, "This is a wonderful life, but it's not the life of my destiny. The life of my destiny is to be in the walls of covenant that God has ordained for me and my people in Jerusalem. Those walls are broken down, and I need to do something about that because the fame of my God is at stake!" Nehemiah had a good life in Babylon, but the good was the enemy of the best.

So how did he continue, in the midst of all this attack? And how do you and I find the strength to move on and not be stopped or delayed in fulfilling our own rebuilding?

Nehemiah's first response was prayer.

"Hear, O our God, for we are despised; turn their reproach on their own heads, and give them as plunder to a land of captivity!... for they have provoked You to anger before the builders" (vv. 4-5).

Nehemiah recognized that ultimately this was God's battle—it was not his own battle, nor was it the battle of the people of Judah.

As you tune into His voice—the frequency of Heaven—you begin to focus and align less with what your enemy is doing and more with what God is doing for you.

Did you know that your battle for your vision and dreams is not yours alone, but God's?

God has a GOOD plan for your life—a plan of purpose, destiny, and fulfillment. God takes it personally when the enemy comes to "steal, kill and destroy" (John 10:10) what God has put in place for you.

So when you set yourself to break free from your past and rebuild a better future, you are literally coming into cooperation and covenant with God Himself—the ultimate ally! How amazing! God Himself is fighting for you. And as you tune into His voice—the frequency of Heaven—you begin to focus and align less with what your enemy is doing and more with what God is doing for you.

Prayer is an invitation to a greater perspective.

It is an invitation to come up higher, to come in deeper, and to see and perceive the eternal in the midst of the temporal. Sure, there are things happening in the natural world— all kinds of things that can seem basic and mundane and frustrating.

But swirling around all of that is the eternal realm, where the Spirit of God is working out purpose and destiny in the midst of the smallest details. Prayer invites us to cooperate with God. To align our spirit with His Spirit.

Nehemiah didn't move in his own anger, but he invoked the righteous anger of the Lord against those who opposed the project: "...they have provoked *You* to anger..."

Our perspective truly changes when we realize a few crucial realities.

God is sovereign. Whatever is happening against me—God is (at least for this moment) allowing. And it will ultimately result for my good. This doesn't mean that we have to stay trapped in a circumstance, or that we become fatalists who don't "push back" against negativity in life. Not at all. But we engage in the battle from a place of ultimate confidence knowing that in the realm of the Spirit, the outcome is already decided, and we WIN. As long as we don't give up, as long as we don't stop looking upwards to Heaven, we cannot lose. There can be momentary setbacks and even things that look like terrible losses, but ultimately, victory is assured.

We need to get some backbone in our prayers again like Nehemiah did in this passage, like David did in many psalms, and like many others did throughout the Scripture. Once Nehemiah invoked the Lord's judgment on *His* enemies, the pressure was off Nehemiah's shoulders, and he could focus on his assignment and leave the rest to the Lord.

Notice that the first thing Nehemiah did when facing this opposition was not to call a committee meeting or check the bank account to see how things were financially. He didn't get a list of all the provisions they had. He didn't call for the wisdom of man.

Nehemiah realized that what was at stake was not something in the natural, but that it was a spiritual battle over covenant—a covenant that God had made. And so his FIRST response was prayer.

Nehemiah knew they had gotten as far as they had on the strength of prayer, and he was determined to continue in the same way they had begun. On the strength of his own wisdom and strategy, the plan was doomed to fail; on the strength of God's wisdom and strategy, the plan was destined to succeed.

DID YOU KNOW?

Waves of Return: Nehemiah was not present in the first large company of Israelites who returned to Judah from Persia. Zerubbabel, a righteous man, was the grandson of King Jehoiachin of Judah and was the leader of the first group. It is believed that Nehemiah became governor of Judah after him.

INTERCESSION THAT WORKS

After Nehemiah petitioned the Lord in response to the opposition on behalf of the builders, something very significant took place. It is so simple, however, that it is easy to overlook the crucial importance of this step in the rebuilding process.

After he prayed and gave the situation to the Lord, in verse 6 it says, *"So we built the wall…"*

In other words, he prayed. *And then—in faith—he worked.*

Even though everything was still the same in the natural, they immediately returned to the task at hand, trusting God for the breakthrough they had asked for. There was no time to lose! What's the lesson?

Do not let the rumblings of the enemy take you off your task.

You can spend all your time running after every negative report, every threat, every piece of slander, every problem. *Don't.* Be confident of your position in God and press forward. The answers and truth of a situation are proved over the long haul, not in fighting momentary, never-ending skirmishes.

So often the enemy would have you running around in circles chasing him, looking for demons around every corner. I believe firmly in the reality of the influence of dark powers in the natural world and in the importance of spiritual warfare. But along with prayer, I believe that the greatest spiritual warfare that we can do is to get up in the morning, day after day, in long and hard toil at times, and continue to put one foot in front of the other until we see the fulfillment of God's promise.

The enemy is not afraid of people who *only* pray and are not willing to act. But if you continue to get up and keep going, even in the worst conditions, you are a dangerous threat to the powers of darkness—because you are someone who believes that prayer can actually cause a shift in circumstances for those who have the tenacity to continue.

Proverbs 24:16 says it this way: "For a righteous man may fall seven times and rise again, but the wicked shall fall by calamity." In other words, you

It is not enough to have faith or to intercede. We must be willing to do something about the things we are praying for.

can't keep a good man or woman down! God's answers in our lives are rarely easy. They are almost never instantaneous. But when you have been transformed within by the Spirit of the Lord and have a perseverance and tenacity that simply will never lie down and die, you will then stand with every fiber of your being upon the Word of the Lord. With God's presence upon you and in you, you will have an inner drive to keep going, because you will know that the results are in God's hands and in God's time.

One of the key things we can learn from the Jewish people is this: though they have an utter and unquestioned dedication and commitment to prayer, they also believe that prayer is empty without good deeds (*mitzvot*) to back it up. Adherence to the commands of God at its core has to have an action component to it, or your faith is not real.

In synagogues today, you will usually find a charity box in the center. This is because many congregants will give charity during their prayer. As the Jews are praying for individual and national success, they are already proving that they will act accordingly with what has been entrusted to them.

> **The history of God's dealings with Israel show us that God is looking for a people who will step out in faith *before* they see the breakthrough.**

The book of James deals with this very issue in a passage that is familiar to most of us:

What does it profit, my brethren, if someone says he has faith but does not have works? Can faith save him? If a brother or sister is naked and destitute of daily food, and one of you says to them, "Depart in peace, be warmed and filled," but you do not give them the things which are needed for the body, what does it profit? Thus also faith by itself, if it does not have works, is dead (James 2:14-17).

It is not enough to have faith or to intercede. We must be willing to *do* something about the things we are praying for. Indeed, we should stop praying prayers if we are not willing to become the answer too.

King David was the quintessential model of this trait. On one hand, he was a man of prayer and deep spiritual connection to God, out of which he composed the Psalms. On the other hand, he was a man of action, ready to go to physical battle with his enemies.

The Scriptures are full of examples demonstrating the necessity of action in the expression of faith:

God provided the sacrifice for Abraham to offer on Mount Moriah, but Abraham had to build the altar and make every preparation to slay his son Isaac *before* the answer came.

God parted the waters of the Red Sea, but Moses had to stretch out his rod and Nachshon of Judah had to get his feet wet *before* the waters began to move.

When coming into the Promised Land, God caused the Jordan River to part for the people to cross, but the priests and Levites had to set their feet into the waters of the Jordan *before* the dry ground appeared. Joshua and the army of Israel witnessed the power of God bringing the walls of Jericho to the ground, but the people had to march around the city and lift their voices in unison *before* the miracle took place.

The Jewish people and the history of God's dealings with Israel show us that God is looking for a people who will step out in faith *before* they see the breakthrough. As they work toward the answer, every action of their hands and hearts is their intercession in motion—their diligence is the expression of their faith and their continual supplication to the Lord. This is intercession that <u>works</u>; this is intercession that <u>perseveres</u>; this is intercession that <u>lives on</u> to see the miracle.

As mentioned above, an example used very often in Jewish society to illustrate this quality is a *midrash* (rabbinical interpretation) about Nachshon Ben Aminadav. As the Israelites

> God delights in inhabiting *ordinary* lives and causing them to be part of His destiny for them.

found themselves trapped between the sea and the Egyptians, they began to argue about the next step to take.

The rabbis tell us that Nachshon Ben Aminadav from the tribe of Judah stepped forward into the sea and continued to walk deeper and deeper until the water reached his nostrils. It was then that God, seeing this faith-filled action, split the sea for the entire nation.

ORDINARY HEROES

There are numerous stories of people in the Bible just like Nehemiah, stories we have read many times over. Stories of ordinary people just like you and me. They faced hunger, thirst, discouragement, danger, fear, and countless other intense situations and difficulties.

It is easy to put our heroes from Scripture on a pedestal, thinking that they were above all the low-level pitfalls that we encounter so often in our lives. We are quick to assume, "Surely they could never have been discouraged when they had seen God's mighty deliverances in Israel!"

But though they lived in a different time, these men and women from the Bible faced all the same types of quagmires that you and I face, and they had to work through doubts and insecurities just like we do. There was nothing special about them, and there is nothing special about us today—just the presence and power of the God who resides inside of us.

God delights in inhabiting *ordinary* lives and causing them to be part of His destiny for them. God delights in connecting with *ordinary* people in *ordinary* situations and using them to be part of the transforming of history that is taking place before their very eyes! You may feel insignificant, but you don't know who you are or what God is about to do through you!

If we as the Church would stop confusing ministry with microphones or pulpits, we would recognize that the same God that rests on famous Christian leaders, both past and present, is the same God that resides in us and empowers us to be His servants in the world around us. It is the same Spirit that raised Jesus from the dead who now lives in us. Therefore, just like Nehemiah and Joshua and David and all the prophets... just like Christian leaders in the Reformation, in the Great Awakenings, in the great revivals of history, and in the present day... you are dangerous to the forces of darkness! God wants you to *rumble* in the midst of your enemies! No matter what you are up against, it is not the time to shrink back in fear or question your own qualifications.

For whom [God] foreknew, He also predestined to be conformed to the image of His Son, that He might be the firstborn among many brethren. Moreover whom He predestined, these He also called; whom He called, these He also justified; and whom He justified, these He also glorified (Romans 8:29-30).

You might be saying, "I don't have influence, I'm not a global leader," but as I often say when speaking to believers, "Who was Billy Graham's Sunday School teacher?" That unnamed, unknown, uncelebrated person likely did not have the slightest idea that he or she was helping to form one of the foremost, influential leaders of the body of Christ in history.

You just don't know the impact that you could be having—even when you are least aware of it! You don't know into what "trumpet" you are sowing your deposit of the Word of the Lord—to raise up a vessel that will be mighty in God's hands. Your life has influence. Your life matters. Whether you are 18 or 81, God has a plan and destiny for you and has appointed you to make a difference in His Kingdom.

THE ISSUE ISN'T THE ISSUE

I want to encourage you today to take a God-sized perspective on challenges that are in front of you. You may have prayed, "God, use me! Lord, I want my life to be pleasing to You—I want to serve You! God, I want to live for You!" And then just a short time later, you didn't understand why you were already facing demonic opposition from the forces of darkness and everything seemingly was going wrong. But do you think that your prayer didn't become known in the spiritual realm?

Don't allow yourself to give in to the discouragement of the enemy. Don't give in to Sanballat's threats. Opposition is confirmation! You simply just became a target because you became dangerous to the enemy. There is an assignment from the enemy against your life, but greater is He who is in you than he who is in the world (1 John 4:4), and His plans for you are greater.

Whatever issue you're facing today *really isn't about that issue.* If you are in the midst of a battle over sickness or physical symptoms, it's really a battle over the covenant of healing that you have with God. If you have a prodigal son or daughter in your family, the battle is over whether the covenant of household salvation applies to your life. You're battling for the covenants of God—that's what you are battling over.

In his battle, Nehemiah's first response was prayer—and in our situations today, our first response must be prayer. If there was more prayer and less talk in the Church in America, we would be a lot closer to where God wants us to be as a people! God is looking for a Nehemiah people whose first response is prayer—and then who add action to their prayers, partnering with God to become the answer to the prayers that they prayed.

FOR FURTHER STUDY:

1. List a time when you experienced opposition from a Sanballat-type figure in your life but were able to overcome. How did you push past the difficulty?

_____

_____

_____

2. Read Habakkuk 2:2-3. Rewrite the four principles of rebuilding, taken from this passage, that are listed in this chapter. Which principle applies the most to you right now as a next step in your own circumstances?

_____

_____

_____

_____

3. What was Nehemiah's first response to the intimidation and opposition he received? How would this same response from you make an impact in your own present situation?

_____

_____

_____

4. Think of someone in your life whom you can encourage to fulfill their life purpose. What is one tangible way you can reach out to encourage that person this week?

_____

_____

_____

CHAPTER 6

THE WEB OF ATTACK

DON'T BE A TOBIAH (WHO'S HE?)

"One ought never to turn one's back on a threatened danger and try to run away from it. If you do that, you will double the danger. But if you meet it promptly and without flinching, you will reduce the danger by half."

—Winston Churchill,
British statesman and prime minister[10]

After we encounter Nehemiah's nemesis, Sanballat, we meet Tobiah the Ammonite. Tobiah is Sanballat's "right-hand henchman."

In what seems like nearly every Marvel superhero movie, every story of good and evil out there, the main character, the protagonist—the Nehemiah—is opposed by a villain, the antagonist—the Sanballat. But in almost every story, the antagonist has a little evil sidekick who serves no other purpose than to agree with everything Sanballat says—that is Tobiah.

Along with every Sanballat comes a Tobiah.

You see, many of us talk about "strongholds" or "principalities," but we fail to recognize how they manifest and operate in the natural world. A stronghold is, simply put, a deeply ingrained pattern of thinking. A thought pattern. Repeated over, and over, and over again, either in one person (an individual stronghold) or in multiple people (a stronghold in a nation or people group).

How did Hitler turn the Nazis into the most deadly force of Jew hatred in history? By repeating lie after lie and finding others to come into agreement with him and to repeat those lies. So while in one way Tobiah is a pathetic and weak creature, on the other hand, he is a very dangerous "useful idiot," because his parroting and affirmation of Sanballat begins to create a web of deception in others.

In other words, people much more easily doubt, question, and challenge ONE voice, than they do TWO voices.

We see this play out in modern media every single day. "Talking heads" are put on the TV screen to try to lead us to believe that there is a diversity of opinion present. But a discerning listener will immediately see that the panel are all reading from the same playbook. They are simply there to affirm the overall ideology of the host program or network. This is how the masses are slowly but easily deceived and controlled—one "Tobiah" at a time.

THE NON-ORIGINAL SIDEKICK

The character Tobiah has no original thoughts to bring to the table, no vision or aspirations of his own—he just gets his security and acceptance from coming into agreement with the agenda of the evil

> **Tobiah is always looking for a vulnerable place (in you) where he can find an evil report that he can easily come into agreement with.**

ringleader. Tobiah draws his identity from identifying with an evil report.

After Sanballat's mocking words in Nehemiah 4:2 ("What are these feeble Jews doing?"), look what is described in the next verse:

Now Tobiah the Ammonite was beside him, and he said, "Whatever they build, if even a fox goes up on it, he will break down their stone wall" (v. 3).

Make no mistake, it is far easier to move into a place of mocking or bullying if someone else takes the first shot. This is what we see operating in Tobiah as he emerges on the scene. He is the one who adds fuel to the fire that is already burning. He is not the one who originates the opposition, but he adds critical mass to it so that it begins to pick up momentum.

In your own life, Tobiah is always looking for a vulnerable place (in you) where he can find an evil report that he can easily come into agreement with, just so that he can feel included and heap his own insults on you. But even though he has little strength of his own, his impact is through the power of agreement—if you are not strong in the word that God has given you and continually renew your mind in His truth.

As God admonished Cain, "If you do what is right, will you not be accepted? But if you do not do what is right, sin is crouching at your door; it desires to have you, but you must rule over it" (Genesis 4:7, NIV). This warning is just as applicable today as it was then.

You need to prepare yourself inwardly for the feeling of when the evil sidekick joins the opposition and, all of a sudden, you feel outnumbered. Then even more, you will need to remind yourself of the clarity of what God said to you in order to withstand the sharpness of the attack. It can be relatively easy to dismiss one attacker from your thoughts, but when you find out that someone ELSE is joining in, it can start to feel overwhelming. It can easily lead you to despair.

You can't do anything about Sanballat, because he is always going to be there. It is a "given" for anyone who has ever made a decision to serve God and to be an active part of God's Kingdom advancing. You also can't do anything about the Tobiahs who join the insults—those who form the coalition of evil voices that Sanballat assembles around himself.

However, no matter how many enemies are coming against you, make a decision today in your heart that you will never be a Tobiah—not in regard to what the enemy is trying to speak over your own life, and not towards someone else's life and calling. Be someone who lives in agreement with Heaven's report, not the enemy's schemes, about yourself or anyone else.

> **No matter how many enemies are coming against you, make a decision today in your heart that you will never be a Tobiah—not in regard to what the enemy is trying to speak over your own life, and not towards someone else's life and calling.**

THE POWER OF ACCUSATION

In the award-winning 1992 film *A Few Good Men,* Tom Cruise plays the role of Lieutenant Daniel Kaffee, a JAG lawyer who is tasked with the defense of two U.S. Marines who have been unjustly accused of murder at the military base at Guantanamo Bay in Cuba, and who are facing a court-martial for their alleged actions.

The power of the false accusation is on full display as the plot unfolds through the legal proceedings, in the attempt from the legal defense to bring justice on behalf of the accused Marines. At the climax of the film, Colonel Nathan Jessup, famously played by Jack Nicholson, finally admits under intense questioning that he ordered the violent Code Red "discipline" that led to the death of the Marine and is arrested. The two Marines under trial, though discharged from duty, are acquitted of the murder charges.

In order for justice to be served in the story, Cruise's character Kaffee and those working on the case have to take a stand against the lie that was masquerading through tactics of intimidation. Standing on the side of truth is not always the easiest—in fact it is often more difficult in the short term. But being a Tobiah and agreeing with the enemy's accusation only brings destruction and harm, to the accused and also to the accuser.

ALLIANCES OF DOUBT

In Genesis 3, when the enemy came to Adam and Eve and questioned, *"Did God really say...?"*, he began to plant the seed of doubt and accusation against God within their minds. He was looking to build alliances around the idea that what God had said was not true—he was looking for agreement.

The power of agreement doesn't only work in the Kingdom of God. It works in the kingdom of darkness as well, which is why we need to be on our guard.

When you start out to become a wall builder, you can be sure that the enemy will come against you to try to derail you from your divine mission. Don't take the bait of his deceptive and accusatory words. Be strong in prayer and intercession like Nehemiah was, and rise up to do the work before you.

Sanballat may have been there to bring an evil report against Nehemiah, but it was when Tobiah *came into agreement* with the report that the evil work of the enemy was strengthened.

Make a decision that you are going to speak life! Decide to never be one who comes into agreement with an evil report, which would strengthen the work of the enemy.

> **Decide to never be one who comes into agreement with an evil report, which would strengthen the work of the enemy.**

Determine to be one who releases faith, who releases life, who releases positive things in the situation, so that when people come around you, they will immediately feel hope and encouragement because the life of God is all around you and working through you. Don't be overwhelmed when Tobiah appears at Sanballat's side, and never move in the spirit of Tobiah!

DON'T PICK UP THE STONE

In John 8, Jesus showed us the power of someone who refuses to take up an accusation against another. In this well-known story, we can see the importance of not coming into agreement with an evil report.

In the story, a crowd of religious men incriminated a woman who had been caught in the act of adultery. They brought her to Jesus to try to win His allegiance to their accusations to have her stoned—and, secretly, to establish a basis for turning their accusations against Jesus Himself.

Jesus refused to be ensnared by their legalistic traps, and He responded, "He who is without sin among you, let him throw a stone at her first" (John 8:7). Convicted by His words, all the accusers departed, leaving the woman free from their malicious plans.

Jesus applied the authority of grace and forgiveness toward the woman, saying to her,

> *"'Woman, where are those accusers of yours? Has no one condemned you?' She said, 'No one, Lord.' And Jesus said to her, 'Neither do I condemn you; go and sin no more'"* (vv. 10-11).

What is astounding in this account is that the men who accused the woman were most likely in the right. But Jesus was less concerned about being in the "right" and more concerned about living in the Truth.

What is more, Jesus knew personally what it was like to face the reality of an angry mob trying to kill Him—He had delayed coming to Jerusalem, knowing that there were those who sought to take His life. Even in this hostile environment, Jesus was not about to come into agreement with the religious leaders' accusations, because He knew that the truth of His Father's redemption was more powerful than the lie of the enemy's accusation.

It only took one person, one voice, to stop the tsunami of accusation. One person who refused to come into agreement with the negative report broke the cycle.

This was by no means the only time that Jesus resisted the enemy's plans to ensnare Him with manipulative and accusatory words. At the very outset of His ministry, Jesus faced the enemy's temptations head-on when He was at a point of physical weakness — fasting and praying in the wilderness (Matthew 4). He passed the test with flying colors because He knew the power of the Truth to combat the lies of the enemy. From the beginning, Jesus had made the decision that He would not come into agreement with the enemy's words, no matter how enticing they were.

DID YOU KNOW?

Post-Exile Prophets: The prophet Haggai and his younger contemporary Zechariah were both among those who returned to Judah before Nehemiah arrived. In partnership with Zerubbabel's leadership, their words urging the people to persevere paved the way for Nehemiah's arrival and the effectual establishment of worship in the restored Second Temple.

Jesus later stated this of the enemy and his duplicitous ways: "…for the ruler of this world is coming, and he has nothing in Me" (John 14:30). Because Jesus had put up a guard against the mindsets of the enemy, those negative thought patterns could not penetrate

Him nor alter the purpose that He was walking in—the purpose given by the Father.

Today when we encounter similar types of lies and accusations, we must likewise stand against them and refuse to come into agreement with the evil report. If the stone is a stone of accusation, don't pick it up. In the places where the enemy would try to entice us to be those who hurl stones of accusation, God has another purpose for us instead: to *become His living stones* in the rebuilding of the walls.

LIVING STONES OF INTERCESSION

In the previous chapter, we talked about the calling to intercession that Nehemiah embraced in his role as a wall builder. In responding to the spirit of Tobiah, we see a powerful aspect of this call to intercession. Where the spirit of Tobiah would have us become *accusers*, God calls us to move in the opposite spirit—to become *intercessors* for others.

In answering God's call as wall builders, we are appointed as living stones in His house:

Coming to Him as to a living stone, rejected indeed by men, but chosen by God and precious, you also, as living stones, are being built up a spiritual house, a holy priesthood, to offer up spiritual sacrifices acceptable to God through Jesus Christ (1 Peter 2:4-5).

In essence, to become a wall builder in God's Kingdom of righteousness (His house), we have to be willing to become stones that make up that wall. In other words, we have to be willing to lay down our lives daily for those around us as intercessors for them.

In the book of Revelation, we see that there are two primary, definitive activities taking place constantly before God's throne in heaven. This becomes enormously important to our everyday lives when we realize its application.

The first activity in Heaven can be seen in Revelation 12:10, which describes Satan as "the accuser of our brethren, who accused them before our God day and night." This activity of *accusation* is reminiscent of the opening scenes of the book of Job, when Satan rails in his accusations before God against Job, a righteous man (Job 1:6-12).

Simultaneously, however, we also see *worship* and *intercession* being lifted before God's throne in Heaven. Revelation 4 describes the continual scene of worship from the living creatures and the elders, who day and night never cease to say, "Holy, holy, holy, Lord God Almighty..." (v. 8) and, "You are worthy, O Lord, to receive glory and honor and power..." (v. 11).

We also see in Revelation 5:8 that the living creatures and elders have with them "golden bowls full of incense, which are the prayers of the saints." Additionally, we know from the book of Hebrews that Jesus is our constant Intercessor before God: "Therefore He is

> **What Jesus did on earth before the accusers of the adulterous woman, He does in Heaven before Satan the accuser of the brethren.**

also able to save to the uttermost those who come to God through Him, since He always lives to make *intercession* for them" (Hebrews 7:25, emphasis added). What Jesus did on earth before the accusers of the adulterous woman, He does in Heaven before Satan the accuser of the brethren.

So we see these two activities warring against each other, constantly, in the unseen heavenly realms, which then manifest on earth: *accusation* from the enemy, and *intercession* from Jesus and the people of God.

Nehemiah was faced with the decision just as we are today: will we come into agreement with the accusations of the enemy against God's people, which brings doubt, discouragement, and fear? Or will we come into agreement with the intercession being lifted before God's throne, which brings life, strength, and blessing? The choice is ours.

BRINGING HEAVEN'S PLANS TO EARTH

In the building of righteous walls, it's important to perceive three roles appointed by God among His people: *prophets* declare the reality that already exists in Heaven, the reality that is to come to earth; *priests* stand in the gap in intercession between what is and what should be; and *apostles* actualize the purposes of God by leading the implementation of these godly plans on the earth.

If Nehemiah did not first live as a priest, standing in the gap in intercession, he could not have moved in the apostolic anointing. This is because the priestly, intercessory call is for ALL believers! First Peter 2:5 calls the people of God collectively "a spiritual house, a holy priesthood," and verse 9 echoes this by calling God's people "a royal priesthood, a holy nation."

> **Will we come into agreement with the accusations of the enemy against God's people, which brings doubt, discouragement, and fear? Or will we come into agreement with the intercession being lifted before God's throne, which brings life, strength, and blessing?**

Some may be gifted as prophets in the role of tearing down false idols, and others may be gifted as apostles who organize and build up the saints, but ALL pray and intercede. To be a living stone in God's house is to be an active participant in what God is doing, which means knowing the Word and being attuned to what God is speaking and doing, through the ongoing, continual activity of prayer and intercession.

Ephesians 2:19-20 tells us that the household of God (God's house) is built on the foundation of the apostles and prophets, with

Jesus Christ Himself being the chief cornerstone. Jesus is the only One who in His life and ministry on earth flowed in ALL the gifts continually; and His example to us is that He did it from the place of continual prayer, so that He would know what the Father was doing. Only then could He bring that spiritual reality to earth.

Verses 21 and 22 summarize the role of the Church, anchored in Jesus our cornerstone, in building the household of God:

in whom the whole building, being fitted together, grows into a holy temple in the Lord, in whom you also are being built together for a dwelling place of God in the Spirit.

As living stones of intercession, you and I are being fitted together to become a holy temple in the Lord. That process brings plenty of opportunities for offense! Being "fitted together" means to have our rough edges chafed and scraped against each other in God's shaping and refining of us, so that what is not His best for us is taken away. It is a painful process, but it is an infinitely rewarding one—and it is what we were created for. Without it the walls of God's house cannot be built, because in His wisdom He has designed the walls of His house to be built in the context of real relationships.

To bring Heaven's plans to earth, we need to receive our direction from the great Architect and Builder, God Himself.

God's plans for building His walls require us to take courage by keeping before us His heavenly perspective. Those who would be wall builders must always keep in mind that there is no natural city without a heavenly city. Hebrews 11:10 says that Abraham, the great father of our faith, "waited for the city which has *foundations, whose builder and maker is God.*"

The way that we build the walls must reflect God's heart of intercession, not the accusation of the enemy. Take courage and stand against the spirit of Tobiah the accuser—decide now to come into agreement with the report of our Master Builder!

FOR FURTHER STUDY:

1. Define the word *stronghold*. How does it take hold within a person or a group of people?

_____

_____

_____

_____

_____

2. What is the power of agreement and why is it so important to be aware of it?

_____

_____

_____

_____

_____

3. Have you ever intentionally (or unintentionally) taken on the role of a "Tobiah" in regards to a situation with another person? Is there anything you still need to make right in that relationship?

_____

_____

_____

_____

4. Read Ephesians 2:21-22. How can you put this scripture into practice with those in your congregation or circle of relationships?

_____

_____

_____

_____

_____

CHAPTER 7

THE HALFWAY POINT

YOUR TESTING GROUND BEFORE BREAKTHROUGH COMES

"Whoever finishes a revolution only halfway, digs his own grave."

—Georg Buchner,
19th-century German writer[11]

Sometimes, the question is not *"Why* do people give up?" but *"When* do people give up?"

Nehemiah and his brave team weathered the constant bombardment of accusation from the enemies around them. They persevered, first by turning to prayer, and then by giving themselves practically and wholeheartedly to the work that was before them.

They made progress, like you will make progress, and then came to the pivotal moment in their mission, which you, too, will reach. The scripture says:

So we rebuilt the wall till all of it reached half its height, for the people worked with all their heart (Nehemiah 4:6, NIV).

> **In every great endeavor for the Kingdom of God, in every personal rebuilding you are working for in your life, there will always be a halfway point, a place of great testing.**

Take special notice of the phrase "half its height."

In this short phrase, we see the decisive moment the group of wall builders reached the most crucial testing point of the entire project. And trust me, fellow rebuilder, it will be your most crucial testing place as well.

Let's review. Nehemiah was the man who came back from exile where he was living in a comfort zone. He was a man motivated to action over the defense of God's covenants, who was facing opposition, and who was responding in prayer. Because he cared about what happened to the city of his forefathers, he embarked on a dangerous few months' journey to reach the land of Judah and assembled a team of builders (who were immediately opposed by enemies). After much hard work, he came to the "half its height" moment in the rebuilding process.

At this moment, Nehemiah faced his most critical battle. I call it the Battle of the Halfway Point.

THE PLACE OF TESTING

In every great endeavor for the Kingdom of God, in every personal rebuilding you are working for in your life (and I would argue, in all worthwhile attempts to make a difference in the world, even by those who don't believe in God), there will always be a halfway point, a place of great testing.

When you receive God's dream and you set out to follow His vision, you are riding a wave of enthusiasm and excitement, and you have energy to move forward with determination on what God has spoken and what you want to accomplish. You have just started to dream! The prophetic confirmation has come! The "Thus saith the Lord" word is over your life, and you are being carried on by the energy and eagerness that's in your heart for the vision. There is no way you're going to stop when you are 10 percent, 15 percent, or 20 percent of the way towards your goal. You are just getting started. There is no way the enemy can take you out at this stage of fulfilling the will and dream of God for your life. You are being carried by the momentum of the "new."

And on the other end, there is also no way you're going to stop when the goal is 85 percent or 90 percent accomplished, because you are almost there! You've worked so hard, and you've worked so long, and the fulfillment is just right ahead of you. Given the advanced stage of the fulfillment of the dream, you will find a way, you will find a solution somehow, because you have come so far and you're almost there.

Even in the discipline of writing this book, and the other books I have written, I can tell you it is easy to START a book, and relatively easy to FINISH a book. The hard part is the writing in the middle! It is the middle of a project, or vision, or change, when

> **Spiritual battlegrounds are littered with the bones of those who stopped not at the beginning, not at the end, but at the halfway point.**

things get really difficult. The middle is when you hit the "wall" and very often, too often, give up.

The enemy and your own weakness can rarely take you out when you're starting or when you're finishing.

But, oh! The testing ground of the Halfway Point!

This is when you have already poured energy and investment and prayer and work and sweat and tears into your vision, but you aren't seeing a lot of results or victories yet. Maybe none at all.

Spiritual battlegrounds are littered with the bones of those who stopped not at the beginning, not at the end, but at the halfway point. This is the place where so many have given up.

In Genesis 11:31, Abram's father Terah took Abram (later Abraham) and his family and left Ur of the Chaldeans to go to the land of Canaan. They first came to Haran and settled there. But then we are then told in the next verse that Terah died at 205 years old in Haran. He set out on a mission but had only gotten halfway. (Ok, we will give him a break because of his age!) But his son Abram would have to take up the mission and finish it.

In this halfway place, we find not only the brokenness of people, but also a pile of the dead dreams of those who did not press through into what God had for them.

But not you.

You will go through this testing ground that will prove the amount of dedication and tenacity and faith that you possess. Don't ever quit there! Get someone in your life to hold you accountable. Find a few trusted friends with whom you can share intimately and honestly. Most importantly, be honest with YOURSELF.

For me, I had to learn in these moments of testing that the battle was not about huge, major decisions; but rather, victory came when I focused on choosing wisely in dozens of "micro-decisions" in a day. I realized these "micro-decisions" (remember, a stronghold is a pattern of thoughts) were the true battleground. A micro-decision can look like...

- Putting down your phone for an hour

- Turning off the TV

- Going for a walk

- Reading your Bible and meditating on it for 15 minutes

- Guarding your speech and not saying every thought that comes to your mind

- Saying "No" to some invitations

- Saying "No" to sugar or unhealthy snacks

- Making a decision to save and invest money every week, even if it is a very small amount.

In his #1 New York Times bestseller *Atomic Habits*, author James Clear brilliantly contends that big change happens one small decision at a time. He says, "Too often we convince ourselves that massive results require massive action." He adds, "The seed of every habit is a single, tiny decision."[12]

For those who are in the midst of battles (and we all are in one way or another), our habits and our way of thinking, moment by moment, are absolutely key. And this is especially true when we are halfway to victory.

The testing ground of the halfway point is where, quite literally, "all hell is breaking loose," because hell has realized that you are serious. You are making progress. You are actually becoming a threat. And hell will access whatever places in your mind and body it has access to, to work against you. Your battle will not only be with exterior forces, but probably more decidedly, with interior forces of negative patterns which have resided there, sometimes going back generations in your family. But you have decided that those chains, those patterns, end with you. They break with you. So you are battling not only for yourself, but for all those who you do not yet realize will benefit from the victory you are winning.

FORGED BY THE BATTLE

I went to college at the University of Valley Forge, Pennsylvania, and almost every day I would drive through Valley

Forge National Park on my way to work. That daily drive, especially in the winter, passing the small log huts that remain to this day, became a powerful reminder of these vital truths.

When General George Washington and his Continental Army stumbled into Valley Forge a week before Christmas in 1777, the weariness of losing a number of battles in the Revolutionary War was setting in. Exhausted, the 12,000 men (as well as several hundred women and children) encamped at Valley Forge for six months until June, housed in log huts that the army had to construct. Each day over those winter months forged a daily testing ground for them individually and as a unit.

The mental and physical battle the troops faced at Valley Forge was a daunting one—arguably even more challenging than their battles against the British army. But without the encampment at this stark location, they almost certainly would not have won the war.

The obstacles they faced were many. They had just lost the fledgling nation's capital of Philadelphia to the British, and morale was low. Personal attacks against the capability of General Washington himself were coming from lawmakers in the Continental Congress. In addition, the fierce elements of winter, the deadly scourge of disease, and the unforgiving scarcity of provisions and supplies tested their ability to endure.

By the time they broke camp in the spring of 1778, approximately 2,000 men had died from the conditions. But those remaining had become a more united, trained, and disciplined army that was significantly better equipped to face the challenges ahead. Because of the new military training implemented by their leadership and their own individual choices in the process, they emerged from their halfway point with new strength for the assignment ahead of them.[13]

And we as Americans are still talking about it today, daily reaping the benefits of their perseverance two and a half centuries later. Would there be an America today if Washington had given up at Valley Forge?

Would there be a Jerusalem today if Nehemiah had given up? Would there be an Israel? Would the Jewish people still exist as a people? Surely Nehemiah understood his task was great and important, but who knows if he could have understood that all of biblical and Jewish history was literally hanging in the balance with the battle he was fighting.

So it is with you.

I am not saying that a nation is going to rise or fall based on your breakthrough. But I am also not saying that it won't! Recent scientific discoveries have shown us the truth of the "butterfly effect"—the cosmic reality that somehow, each of our individual lives and stories have an impact, like ripples from a stone thrown in a lake, that extend far beyond our lifetimes and far beyond our understanding. My close friend Mark Gerson, the best-selling author, thought leader, and philanthropist, often reminds us, "As the Torah tells us in Deuteronomy 11:26, 'See, I have put before you a blessing and a curse.' The 'see' is in the singular, but the 'you' is in the plural—teaching us even seemingly isolated and minor actions have wide-ranging and unpredictable effects that affect lots of people and lots of things."

God alone knows the full extent of your battle and the full meaning of your victory.

If you have been running well but are now facing increasing difficulties in your journey, press on past your halfway point. Allow the dream and God's Word over you to test and refine you, so that you will come forth as gold (see Job 23:10). God's Word is true and will sustain you through to victory, one step, one micro-decision at a time.

ALL THEIR HEART

The other absolutely key phrase I want to highlight from Nehemiah 4:6 is this… "the people worked with all their heart."

What does it mean to be "whole-hearted?"

It is, for sure, a vital key to your success and victory.

The Bible says, "A double minded man is unstable in all his ways" (James 1:8, KJV).

The prophets of Israel, especially Elijah, constantly confronted the people about their inability to be faithful and loyal to their core beliefs and worship of the One God. As Elijah said to the people of Israel, "How long will you falter between two opinions? If the Lord is God, follow Him; but if Baal, follow him" (1 Kings 18:21). Before we judge them too quickly, however, isn't it the same with us?

We say we want to rebuild and restore Broken Places in our lives. Relationships, our physical health, our business, our emotional wellbeing—whatever it is. But we have been deeply and physically scripted through neurons and synapses and neural pathways in our brains to reject the very thing that we say we want to embrace. We are divided, and so often at war with ourselves.

The Apostle Paul seemed to wrestle with this in an especially intense way.

> *For I know that good itself does not dwell in me, that is, in my sinful nature. For I have the desire to do what is good, but I cannot carry it out. For I do not do the good I want to do, but the evil I do not want to do—this I keep on doing. Now if I do what I do not want to do, it is no longer I who do it, but it is sin living in me that does it* (Romans 7:18-20, NIV).

To work with "all our heart" we have to rewire our heart, mind, and physical body into the better patterns—the sacred strongholds—which will bring life, not death.

When we begin to move in health individually, we are able to share that divine spark with those around us. Peer pressure works positively, not only negatively. As Nehemiah's group banded together, they were able to draw their strength from God and from each other to persevere in the midst of heavy criticism and attack. You need to work "with all your heart." You need to find within yourself the dream, the goal, the vision… as well as the power to focus, unite, and harness your mind, body, and spirit for its completion.

> **The people of Judah were able to see the big picture of what they were doing together, which gave them the strength to press through the challenges they were facing.**

Stirred by Nehemiah's leadership and example and bolstered by the words that God had spoken over them, the people of Judah worked with *all* their heart. I believe that they were able to see the big picture of what they were doing together, which gave them the strength to press through the formidable but momentary challenges they were facing.

By rebuilding the location where the presence of God had rested over Israel, they were welcoming again the glory of God to Jerusalem. They were building a resting place for the presence of God.

As it was for the people of Judah, there should be nothing that is more motivational to us than the glory of God, the Spirit of God, and the presence of the living God. What does it look like when God rests in your home? In your marriage? In your children? In your church? In your business? The breakthrough in your personal life

> **What we encounter in this point of the story is the monumental difference between being *churchgoers* and being *wall builders*.**

WILL result in an increase of the presence of God in those who surround you.

What we encounter in this point of the story is the monumental difference between being *churchgoers* and being *wall builders*. There are millions upon millions of churchgoers in our nation and around the world, but how many committed, godly *wall builders* do we have in our generation?

The difference between these two types of believers is the difference between being spectators in life and becoming a collective force to be reckoned with. The difference is whether or not we choose to be an active part of the Kingdom of God as it advances first *in* us, and then *through* us.

Churchgoers, more often than not, give up on the call to rebuild the walls at the halfway point. Something happens. A church split. A moral failure of a leader. The "cares of this world" pressing in on them. They hit a wall spiritually and lose their zeal. Maybe they keep attending "for the kids," or because the church has become their friend group; but they are no longer truly wrestling with a sense of calling and destiny over their lives.

They are likely to pull up their roots and start over somewhere else, aimlessly and thoughtlessly feeling, "I must need a new church," rather than looking within themselves for the well of life.

Wall builders, on the other hand, have allowed the difficulties that they have faced to form something inside them, so that they will never give in to the threats of the enemy. They push *through* the halfway point to the victory on the other side. If they find themselves in a spiritual desert, they dig their own well.

Banded together in this hour like Nehemiah's company, we need to lift our vision higher!

DID YOU KNOW?

Unusual Chronology: The books of Ezra and Nehemiah, which are part of Israel's post-exilic era, appear in the Bible *before* the prophetic literature that led up to the exile. Ezra and Nehemiah also are placed directly before the book of Esther, which actually pre-dates them both as it took place during the captivity. Even more unusual in sequence, after Esther comes the book of Job, which should be located chronologically parallel to Genesis at the beginning of the Bible!

> Count the cost of the halfway point before you get there. Decide when you start that stopping is never an option.

THE HIGHER CALL

Our world needs the body of Christ to view and understand ourselves as an inter-generational, international assembly of people who make a united, sustained impact on the world around us. Instead of running from the battle, we should learn to embrace it when God allows us to go through trials and difficulties—which will only make us stronger. Those very things will provide us the opportunity to rise above and press through to a new place in our walk with God.

We need to answer the high call of God on our lives to be His representatives in the world around us—in excellence, in leadership, and to advance the Kingdom of God... to be the head and not the tail, to be above and not beneath (see Deuteronomy 28:13), to be passionate leaders and not merely followers in the regions where God has placed us. But it is going to take the Nehemiah heart to rebuild the broken walls in this generation. Count the cost of the halfway point before you get there. Decide when you start that stopping is never an option.

Nehemiah and his team broke through the test of the halfway point—because they worked with all their heart. When opposition increased, they didn't panic. Instead, they prayed and acted decisively:

But when Sanballat, Tobiah, the Arabs, the Ammonites and the people of Ashdod heard that the repairs to Jerusalem's walls had gone ahead and that the gaps were being closed, they were very angry. They all plotted together to come and fight against Jerusalem and stir up trouble against it. But we prayed to our God and posted a guard day and night to meet this threat (Nehemiah 4:7-9, NIV).

"Standing in the gap" has never been more literal. And again, here is the pattern prayer AND action. They prayed AND posted a guard.

The nature of these "day and night" watchmen is that they laid hold of the Lord's purposes even when it was inconvenient—even when it was 3 a.m. and raining outside. There was a wholehearted commitment from the people to be involved in a community that was building the work of God 24 hours a day, 7 days a week, 365 days a year.

There could be no more evident example of "watchmen on the wall" than the rotating guards that Nehemiah posted on the walls of Jerusalem. They were Isaiah 62 in living color:

I have posted watchmen on your walls, Jerusalem; they will never be silent day or night. You who call on the Lord, give yourselves no rest, and give him no rest till he establishes Jerusalem and makes her the praise of the earth (vv. 6-7, NIV).

> **Guards in Nehemiah's day had to be vigilant, dedicated, focused, and determined. They had to put their own preferences aside in order to be at God's disposal.**

These guards in Nehemiah's day had to be vigilant, dedicated, focused, and determined. They had to put their own preferences aside in order to be at God's disposal for the assignment that He had for them to fulfill. They could not afford to be petty, and they didn't have the time to be offended; they were moving together and had to take seriously their role in the rebuilding of the wall, or all could be lost.

Then and now, God is looking for watchmen who will watch over Jerusalem in prayer, warding off every spiritual attack and also helping to defend Jerusalem in the natural against her enemies. Watchmen lift their voices when they see danger coming; they mobilize the people of God to fight the battle; and they use tactical strategies to defend the city of Jerusalem, including exposing the lies that have been levied against her.

In the same way that we must watch over Jerusalem in prayer and in active support for the land of Israel, God also calls us to watch over our own families, cities, and regions. To be effective in our assignment, we must be informed both of what the Bible says to us and also the strategies of darkness that manifest in acts of aggression against the people of God and the covenants of God. You are appointed by God to be an intercessor, a watchman in prayer and action, and a defender of truth wherever you go.

Now is the time, urgently, to get plugged in and give ourselves fully to the work of the Lord in our churches and communities, in this critical hour when faith is under assault worldwide. It's time for us to have a mindset shift, to be ready to live from the place where God Himself resides within us. There should be a fountain of praise that is ready to come out of each one of us at a moment's notice, from the heart of a world changer who realizes that the world changes only when he or she first changes within.

BEFORE A WATCHING WORLD

In society today, probably as never before, the world is watching the Church. They are looking to see if we are the "real deal," if we are pressing forward into the way things *should* be, not just the way things *are*. The world is often more perceptive of the Church than we may realize, seeing through our spiritual smokescreens to assess our authenticity. Do we really love our neighbors, or do we just love them if they line up with our set of beliefs and life principles?

Too often, what should be present in the Church is so different than the faltering testimony of the way things really are. The watching world is looking for the authentic, true Kingdom of God—something that has the power to shape and transform lives. They are looking for walls of safety that speak of the expression of covenantal relationships in the people of God.

Will we be a people who press through into victory or who give up at the halfway point? The mandate from Isaiah 62:6-7 to live as watchmen on the wall is a divine invitation to a life of impact, truth, and breakthrough.

Day and night, night and day... may we be those who answer that call.

May we pass the test of the halfway point and never be silent, even in the face of great opposition.

FOR FURTHER STUDY:

1. Think of a project large or small that you gave up on when you were halfway through. What can you learn from that experience?

_____

_____

_____

_____

_____

2. What is one "dead dream" that you know you need to pick back up again?

_____

_____

_____

_____

3. In the account of Nehemiah, it says the people worked with "all their heart" when they reached the halfway point of building the wall. How can you bring an attitude of wholeheartedness to the places where you are seeking breakthrough?

_____

_____

_____

_____

_____

4. Read Isaiah 62:6-7. What are some key areas of your life that God has given you to watch over diligently?

_____

_____

_____

_____

_____

CHAPTER 8

FIGHT FOR YOUR FAMILIES

DISCOVER YOUR WHY THROUGH COVENANT RELATIONSHIPS

"If you want to go fast, go alone. If you want to go far, go together."

— African Proverb[14]

After Nehemiah and the people made the decision to persevere through the testing ground of the halfway point, things did not immediately get any easier. In fact, the exact opposite happened. Up until this point, the opposition Nehemiah had faced was coming almost entirely from their enemies. Now, the opposition began to come also from within.

With things heating up around them, Nehemiah and the builders needed to discover their "why"—the deep inner motivation to find a way through.

> When you are in a spiritual war, the first thing the enemy will attack is your praise.

OPPOSITION ALL AROUND

In this moment of challenge, three groups were bringing a negative report. When it rains, it pours! Let's look at each of them individually.

1. The first group was the people of Judah. Look at Nehemiah 4:10:

Then Judah said, "The strength of the laborers is failing, and there is so much rubbish that we are not able to build the wall."

The people of Judah were Jews, who by the definition of the very name of their tribe were called to praise (see Genesis 29:35)! *Judah* said the strength of the laborers was giving out. Judah was supposed to report about what *God* said about the situation, through high praise—not to lower their gaze to what was happening in the natural. As a result, the people of Judah lost their confession.

When you are in a spiritual war, the first thing the enemy will attack is your praise. If the enemy can silence your praise, he's already won the battle—because God *inhabits* the praises of His people, and it's the presence of God that is at stake in the situation.

When we praise, it creates room for God to move. When in spite of the roadblocks we are facing, we choose to worship in that very place of difficulty, it expands the capacity for God to act in a situation. As a people, we must always be a worshipping house, a praising house, a praising people—because there is victory in our praise!

In the biblical account, the people of Judah took their eyes off the covenantal promise of God and shifted their focus onto the situation, looking at all the things they were up against. But none of us as God's people are called to report on the way things are. We are called to declare those things that are *not* as though they were (see Romans 4:17) and to give the report of the Lord. There is power in the words we speak and declare. We manifest what we focus on and what we speak out. Judah began to look at the report of what currently *was*, instead of God's perspective to transform the situation. Don't let your inner Judah lose your confession of faith!

2. The second group bringing a negative report was an alliance of Nehemiah's enemies. They had been there all along but were becoming more vocal and adamant. They began to intensify their approach when they saw that the builders were determined to continue. Verse 11 says:

And our adversaries said, "They will neither know nor see anything, till we come into their midst and kill them and cause the work to cease."

The escalation of the situation was so intense that the builders were now receiving death threats for what they were doing. No longer was this just a threat against their work—now it was also against their very lives.

3. The third group, incredibly, were the Jews who were living in the surrounding areas.

So it was, when the Jews who dwelt near them came, that they told us ten times, "From whatever place you turn, they will be upon us" (v. 12).

Imagine the scene for a moment: who said these words? Jews. Whom did they say it to? Also Jews. Let's not forget that Nehemiah and the people he was rebuilding the wall with were Jews! The Jews surrounding Judah were so deep into agreement with the evil report that they aired their doubts against the Jewish builders *ten times over!*

Nehemiah, by the vision he pioneered, had brought a company of people back to rebuild the wall and to bring safety to the Jews. But the very people he was trying to help, the very family that he was laboring to assist, the very ones for whom he was pouring out his energy—the very ones for whom he had left the comfort, the security, the opulence, and the extravagance of the palace because he was concerned for their safety—*they were the ones* who began to speak against him.

For Nehemiah, this was perhaps his most daunting challenge of all, as his reputation and character were being questioned by his own people. If you're going to be a wall builder, then you are going to face the test of being misunderstood, blamed, and resented by the very people that you are laboring to love and build up and protect.

> **The test of Nehemiah's heart became:** *Am I doing this for man, or am I doing this for God?*

The test of Nehemiah's heart at that moment became, ultimately: *Am I doing this for man, or am I doing this for God?* This was because all motivation to do anything out of blessing or serving man disappeared in that moment—he had no more motivation from man. Judah had given up, the enemies were attacking, and the surrounding Jews were also coming against him.

Centuries ago when Moses was bringing the people of Israel out of Egypt and towards the Promised Land for the first time, he was attacked and opposed in the same way by the very people that he was leading into God's provision and fulfillment of the promise. Now Nehemiah faced this challenge as he was bringing the Israelites *back* to the Promised Land to rebuild the walls. He faced their complaining, and ten times over, just as Israel had done in the wilderness. And there they were—right at the fulfillment of the promise once again!

Nehemiah stood as a lone figure in his story, holding out against all odds, against every attack… straining and believing and reaching forward to rebuild the walls of Jerusalem.

THE SPEECH OF A LIFETIME

Nehemiah 4:13-14 show his history-making response to these numerous attacks against the rebuilding efforts, and the flagging faith of the wall builders. He addressed the fear and exhaustion of the people head-on:

> *Therefore I stationed some of the people behind the lowest points of the wall at the exposed places, posting them by families, with their swords, spears and bows. After I looked things over, I stood up and said to the nobles, the officials and the rest of the people, "Don't be afraid of them. Remember the Lord, who is great and awesome, and <u>fight for your families</u>, your sons and your daughters, your wives and your homes"* (NIV, emphasis added).

What was Nehemiah's "why" that he discovered in that crucial moment? I believe it was that he was part of a covenant people who had been appointed by God to that land. It would have been so easy for him to feel demoralized and to give way to hopelessness. But he realized that being part of a covenant people meant showing his utter commitment to them and helping them also to discover their "why"—even when the battle was the toughest.

Verses 13 and 14 tell us that he positioned men at the lowest points of the wall, the exposed places where they were open to attack, and then he gathered the people as families and gave them the greatest charge of their lives.

I can just imagine Nehemiah at this defining moment, turning to the people like William Wallace rallying the army of Scotland in *Braveheart*, or Aragorn summoning the courage of the armies of Middle-earth in *The Lord of the Rings*. They had come so incredibly far to get to this do-or-die crossroads… and Nehemiah was going to do everything in his power to keep them from giving up. He said to them, "Remember the Lord, and fight for your families!" (v. 14).

Nehemiah, in the turning point of the story, appealed to the greatest motivator he had at his disposal: he appealed to their covenantal relationship to each other.

He stationed the people *by families* along the walls, posting them with their swords, their spears, and their bows. By doing so, he was positioning them in such a way as to cause them to look into the eyes of their loved ones—and find a new depth of covenantal resolve.

AN INHERITANCE WORTH DYING FOR

Nehemiah put the families in position, not at places where the wall was secure, not at places that were safe, but at places that were vulnerable to an attack—because the enemy had access at that moment to come and exploit those places of fragility. He posted them there by families, not by committees, not by who was strongest and who was weakest, but he posted them by *families*; he brought them there and stood them in position as the battle threatened to rage against them.

DID YOU KNOW?

Story of the Second Temple: The Second Temple was destroyed by General Titus and the Roman army in 70 AD, but that was not the first time that it fell into enemy hands. The story of Hanukkah originated during the second century BC when the Second Temple was overrun by the Seleucid Empire under the King Antiochus IV Epiphanes of Syria, who killed thousands in Jerusalem. Antiochus' men built an altar to Zeus inside the Temple, thus desecrating it. The ensuing Jewish revolt led by the Maccabees cleansed the temple once again, re-dedicating the area once again as a holy place for worship and driving the Syrians out of the city.

In this action, Nehemiah was saying to them, "This is not about a building; this is not about a wall; this is about what kind of world our children will grow up in. Will they survive this battle knowing the importance of the land of our forefathers, or will they see a lack of resolve in us to fight for our God-given homeland?"

For Nehemiah, it was not an option to turn back. It would be far worse to return to a place of forfeiting their inheritance than to lose their lives in defending that inheritance. It would be like the children of Israel going back to Egypt when God was promising them a land of their own.

This portion of the story of Nehemiah reminds me of one of the most impactful places for me when I travel to Israel: the massive rocky plateau known as Masada in the Judean desert in Southern Israel, overlooking the nearby Dead Sea. This location was made into an opulent desert fortress by Herod the Great, the Judean king who reigned from 37 BC to 4 BC as a powerful representative of Caesar.

During the Great Jewish Revolt against Roman oppression (66-73 AD), a large band of several hundred Jewish Zealots and their families took refuge at Masada, making it a Jewish military outpost against the Romans where they prepared for a last stand on behalf of their people.

When the Roman general Flavius Silva laid siege to Masada, the Jewish Zealots courageously held their ground, using their high elevation to fight off the Romans for several months, including fighting back valiantly against a siege ramp and battering ram.

Eventually their defense came to a tragic end when, with a limited amount of resources and weapons, they realized they would no longer be able to keep the Romans at bay. In a shared pact among them, the leaders of the Zealots decided to take their own lives and that of their families, rather than submitting to certain slavery or death at the hand of the Romans.

Although they did not prevail in the physical battle, the Zealots' courageous stand lives on in Jewish history and continues to inspire those who make pilgrimage to Israel today—reminding us of the importance of fighting for our families and banding together as a people through the power of covenant relationships.

UNITY WHERE NEEDED MOST

As Nehemiah positioned the families at the lowest places of the wall, he also broke down a wall between the people. Every individual and family became part of a community reliant on each other in order to protect themselves.

This unity is something that is profoundly lacking in the Western world, including among Western Christians. People need to see the strength of unity as an indispensable weapon against the enemies that are coming against us. In Jewish culture, disagreement and debate are a deep part of daily life and are even promoted in order to stretch the minds of the community of people. Israeli politics, like the rest of the world's, display political parties speaking out against each other's policies and even bad-mouthing each other as individuals.

But when it comes to the protection of the State and People of Israel, the country comes together as one and fights the enemy. There may even be soldiers that disagree with the way the government is fighting a war, but they come together in the trenches and fight as one. They embody the realization that the survival of the nation is a higher priority than individuals' opinions.

There is a puzzling verse in the Bible (Exodus 19:2) that describes the people stationed at Mount Sinai: "And Israel encamped there opposite the mountain." Through a deeper study of the Hebrew language,

> **Unity is not only a powerful tool when fighting darkness; it is also a powerful tool in spreading light.**

we find that the word used here for "encamped" is in singular form, not the plural form that would be expected when describing the entire nation.

The famous medieval rabbi Rashi picks up on this and gives us a wonderful understanding. He comments that as the Israelites were encamped around Mount Sinai for the giving of the Torah, they were as "one person with one heart."[15] They were, for that historical moment in time, individuals, families, and tribes all coming together—unified in their oneness under God and this world-changing moment.

Unity is not only a powerful tool when fighting darkness; it is also a powerful tool in spreading light.

STRENGTH IN THE LOWEST PLACES

For Nehemiah and the people of Judah, the bottom line was that God had made a covenant with them, and that covenant was the foundation on which the people stood as a covenant community. Their relationships were built on the strength of God's promises to them collectively, and this is what was under attack by the enemy.

And if the enemy could take them out through doubt or fear, then the testimony of who God was among them would suffer in the eyes of the nations.

Nehemiah recognized that there was a larger battleground in question at that moment than just his own personal reputation, and he invested his energies into helping those with him to realize what was at stake. They were being attacked as a people, and as a people they must fight. At the lowest and most vulnerable places, he posted them by families to withstand the onslaught against their covenant way of life.

We can truthfully say today that with the invasion of militant secularism, moral relativism, and other forms of radicalism, our regions in America are also at some of the "lowest places" in the wall. The enemy is trying to invade and to establish his control of American society, and God is looking for some wall builders in our nation. God is looking for some to stand at the lowest, exposed places and say, "This is not just about Nehemiah's or my pastor's vision or dream—this is about me being faithful to *my* God and passing on to *my* children the security of a wall that has been rebuilt."

The battle must become personal!

In this hour, you must choose what the priority system of your family will be—a subculture of the world around you, or a Kingdom culture that transcends other priorities. The house of God and the expansion of God's Kingdom must be the priorities of our lives. If we don't fortify the vulnerable places in our regions and communities by advancing the values of the Kingdom as families, the way of life of the next generation will greatly suffer.

> **We need to ask ourselves, what kind of nation will our children inherit?**

We have never been called to be a sub-culture; rather, we have been called to be a *counter-culture* that confronts the kingdom of darkness with the reality of the Kingdom of God. Day and night, this is our responsibility from the Lord.

We need to ask ourselves, what kind of nation will our children inherit? Will we stand against the enemy's onslaught that would seek to remove God's covenant from our society?

STANDING FOR COVENANT

In this fight for our own lives and families, remember what Nehemiah said to the people: "Don't be afraid of them! Remember the Lord, who is great and awesome, and fight!" He exhorted them to hold their ground and to stand courageously for covenant. He urged them to find their "why" by defending the covenant relationships that defined who they were as a people.

Maybe God is speaking to you that there is a wall of covenant that you need to rebuild in your family. It could be a wall in your marriage that has broken down… a wall of a vital, nurturing relationship with a child… or a wall of righteousness protecting your relationship with God. All of these and many other examples could be areas where something good and right in your life has been overrun, and sin has found its way into your life or your family, polluting the stream of your relationship with God or those around you.

In those very places that are broken, I believe God is saying to you, "I want you to rebuild this portion of the wall. You are responsible to pull out of the comfort zone of your life and get intentionally involved in rebuilding this wall of righteousness."

To do so, you have to prepare yourself for the voices of Sanballat and Tobiah. You have to prepare yourself for the crucial halfway point. You have to prepare yourself for when Judah gives out and the spirit of praise seems to be gone from the atmosphere, and you can't find a breakthrough—and when the enemies are surrounding you, and even those that you are laboring for and love and have given yourself for don't understand you. In this moment of challenge, choose to praise God because you are positioned to be a wall builder! You are positioned to shape history in that moment— right there in the most vulnerable places in your life.

After Nehemiah gave the people the charge to fight for their families, a remarkable breakthrough took place. As had so often happened previously throughout Israel's history, God intervened:

And it happened, when our enemies heard that it was known to us, and that God had brought their plot to nothing, that all of us returned to the wall, everyone to his work (Nehemiah 4:15, emphasis added).

We don't know the exact details of what took place between verse 14 and verse 15, but what we do know is that it became evident, even to the *enemies* of the people of Judah, that the people were not going to be deterred, they were not going to give up, and that God Himself had taken action and frustrated the plans of the enemy.

Through perseverance, the greatest victory had been won: under Nehemiah's determined leadership, the people were not shaken from the reality of the purpose for which they had been sent. They remembered the Lord and remembered who they were as a people, which was more powerful than any backbiting, doubt, or strife.

As the people took their stand with renewed strength, knowing *why* they were giving themselves to the effort of rebuilding the walls, God proved that He would take care of the rest. His covenant with them as a people could never be removed, no matter what attack raged against it.

BUILDING IN THE BATTLE

The remarkable testimony that emerged from those who built the wall is a powerful combination of simultaneously living in the midst of the battle and building for the future:

Those who built on the wall, and those who carried burdens, loaded themselves so that with one hand they worked at construction, and with the other held a weapon. Every one of the builders had his sword girded at his side as he built. And the one who sounded the trumpet was beside me (Nehemiah 4:17-18).

The rebuilding project in Jerusalem was anything but a cakewalk. It required great courage and a night-and-day readiness to defend the work from enemies surrounding the area.

This example has been manifested time and again in the modern state of Israel, as those who rebuilt the ancient cities in Israel had to protect their communities vigilantly even while they went through the process of rebuilding.

A modern-day Nehemiah and hero of the faith that I have had the privilege of knowing and working with personally through the years is the indomitable Shlomo Riskin, the Chief Rabbi of Efrat (Ephrata), between Bethlehem and Hebron.

Rabbi Riskin was an extremely successful and distinguished rabbi, the founder of the influential Lincoln Square Synagogue in the Upper West Side of New York City. He was at the top of his career, with impressive opportunities awaiting him, when he decided to leave the well-to-do security of New York City and take his family and immigrate to Israel to help rebuild the fledgling settlement of Efrat.

The stories of the early days of Efrat were right out of the book of Nehemiah. The group of settlers had to post guards to keep their community safe from attacks while they rebuilt the city. There were negative opinions from all around, including parts of the Israeli government, trying to convince Rabbi Riskin not to move ahead with his bold vision. It was difficult work with many challenges along the way and no certainties of success. But a word from Heaven guided and strengthened Rabbi Riskin and his new community, and they knew they had been appointed by the God of Israel to rebuild the ancient walls.

Many other rebuilt communities of Judea and Samaria faced similar circumstances as they worked to make the desert of Israel bloom once again after many years of the land lying neglected and desolate. As they labored together in community, the people of Israel had to add their faith and hard work in order to see the fulfillment of the promise. When fierce opposition arose (as it still does today), the people found deep within themselves the strength of their covenant commitment to each other and to God as a community, to achieve the fulfillment of their dream in their ancient homeland.

The walls that God appoints us to build with our own families in our own communities may look a little different and may not seem on the surface to be anything of biblical proportions like the builders of modern Efrat. But those who carry the heart of a wall builder recognize that ultimately it is not their geographic location or the level of influence that they possess that makes the rebuilding worthwhile.

The section of the wall that God has assigned to you to rebuild right now might only be *one broken relationship*—and after that one more broken place in your life that needs to be repaired. Any lack

> **Opposition will either distract, divide, and defeat you, or it will drive you to covenant resolve.**

of perceived magnitude of the context does not detract from the importance and the God-appointed nature of the rebuilding.

What we can learn from these courageous examples is that opposition will either distract, divide, and defeat you, or it will drive you to covenant resolve.

I have often heard it said by one of my spiritual fathers, Dan Juster, that love in its purest definition is the compassionate identification with others that seeks their good, guided by God's law. It is the commitment to reach out to the one person next to you, on the basis of the strength and truth of God's Word, which is the same for one as it is for 1,000. The value of each human life is the setting, the environment, where God's mercy shines brightly with the beauty of His covenant.

As you seek to be a wall builder on your journey of faith, allow covenant relationships to be the rudder that keeps you in the center of God's purposes. Allow the opposition you encounter to be a strength multiplier, an extra rear motor that propels you forward into your destiny in God. And allow love and compassion to be the sail that unfurls to welcome in the wind of the Spirit to chart the course of your journey ahead.

FOR FURTHER STUDY:

1. Have you ever been opposed by the very people you were trying to help? What advice would you give to someone going through a similar situation?

_____

_____

_____

_____

_____

2. Think of the people in your life whom you would identify as covenant relationships, either family members or others that you are closest to. How can you support their personal journey as well as receive strength personally through those relationships?

_____

_____

_____

_____

_____

_____

3. What are two practical ways you can fight for the good of the next generation coming after you?

_____

_____

_____

_____

4. Is there one "section in the wall"—perhaps a broken-down relationship in your life—that you need to re-engage in? What first step could you make in that process?

_____

_____

_____

_____

_____

_____

_____

CHAPTER 9

REDISCOVERING IDENTITY

ALIGNING YOUR LIFE TO GOD'S CALENDAR
AND TO HIS PEOPLE

"If we find ourselves with a desire that nothing in this world can satisfy, the most probable explanation is that we were made for another world."

—C.S. Lewis,
Christian author and theologian[16]

Nehemiah and his companions returned to rebuild their spiritual Home and nation in Jerusalem. They were not only building the physical walls, but just as importantly, and maybe more importantly, they were recovering and restoring their identity as a people.

You cannot rebuild your marriage, your business, your dreams, without rediscovering and rebuilding YOU. Your inner world is intrinsically connected to the outer manifestation of your life.

Step by step, they began to re-dig the wells of their inheritance. Despite intense opposition, the favor of God was with them and the

> **You cannot rebuild your marriage, your business, your dreams, without rediscovering and rebuilding YOU.**

wall of the city was completed in a miraculous 52 days, on the 25th day of Elul (see Nehemiah 6:15), the sixth month of the biblical calendar year. 52 days. 52 days to change history. Never underestimate the power of a short, focused time to pivot into something powerful, new, and long-lasting.

The children of Israel had been in Babylon, living outside their homeland, calendar, identity, and value system. Sometimes, a crisis takes us "out of alignment." We lose the normal rhythm of worship, values, family, calendar... all of the things that combined, we call "culture."

Interestingly, the etymology of the words *culture* and *cult* point back to the Latin word *cultus*, the definitions of which connote not only cultural customs but also cultivation of land: "care, labor; cultivation, culture; worship, reverence," originally "tended, cultivated."[17] The related Latin *cultura*, by the 1500s also carried the following meaning: "cultivation through education, systematic improvement and refinement of the mind."[18]

In short, *culture* carries with it the meaning of personal and community cultivation (both physical and educational growth), of a way of life, and most importantly, of worship that shapes the community of faith. This is what the people of Judah were tapping into once again in the land of their forefathers when they took concrete action to rebuild the culture of their people.

> **Your personal rebuilding is part of a generational rebuilding.**

Just as Israel and Judah had gotten away from the full manifestation of their roots and culture while living in a foreign land—thus needing to be realigned fully once again—so we as the Church in this era of history are coming back to those same biblical, Hebraic roots, a historic returning which is a massive part of the rebuilding that is happening in this generation. All the biblical rebuilding we are doing today is linked intrinsically to this most important rebuilding project of all time.

Your personal rebuilding is part of a generational rebuilding. Let that sink in. You as an individual are interwoven and interconnected to a greater whole.

As we come out of our own exile in "Babylon"—the place of faulty world and even church systems that have left us spiritually malnourished—we reconnect to our biblical root once again. We find ourselves "grafted in," planted firmly in the truth of God's enduring covenant with His people Israel, and we begin to experience a beautiful restoration of the life that God intended for us. In all our work of building, we must continually heed God's command which says, "Remember that you do not support the root, but the root supports you" (Romans 11:18).

In order to sustain as a community in their resettling of the land under Nehemiah, the people of Judah would need to realign with their biblical roots and way of life that had been commanded by God Himself in the days of Moses and Joshua. Otherwise, their arduous work in rebuilding the wall would be all for naught. In that crucial moment, the vital foundation of their spiritual DNA began to come into full view. Shortly after completing the wall, some remarkable things related to their spiritual heritage began to take place.

DIGGING FOR FAMILY ROOTS

Have you ever been bitten by the "genealogy bug?" I think the majority of people, at some point in their lives, become curious about their ancestors. We want to know where and whom we came from. Sites like Ancestry.com and 23andme.com and others have capitalized on this deeply primal need to know our origin story.

Why? Where does this curiosity come from?

Something deep inside us lets us know that we will not fully understand our present or our future until we more fully understand and reconcile with our past.

I remember a time when I became curious and spent a few months looking into my genealogy. I was amazed to discover that the first recorded "Stearns" to come to America was Isaac Stearns, who sailed in the 1600s on a ship that was originally christened "The Eagle."

As soon as they completed the initial city wall, Nehemiah set about to rediscover family lines. Genealogy. Remember, when the children of Israel first came into the land under Joshua, they were assigned various areas of the land by their tribes. Now, as they returned, Nehemiah realized the importance of reminding the people that they were not disconnected immigrants, but they were actually a family of families, returning to the land of their inheritance. In the time when the scripture tells us that the number of people in the city was still few and the houses had not yet been reconstructed (see description given in 7:4), Nehemiah began to pioneer the effort of establishing the people in the region by their clans.

Nehemiah was now appointed to be the governor of Judah under Artaxerxes, the Persian king. He literally located the Ancestry.com of the day, the registry of family names of those who had returned, and he brought it to the forefront of their awareness as a people.

Then my God put it into my heart to gather the nobles, the rulers, and the people, that they might be registered by genealogy. And I found a register of the genealogy of those who had come up in the first return, and found written in it: "These are the people of the province who came back from the captivity, of those who had been carried away, whom Nebuchadnezzar the king of Babylon had carried away, and who returned to Jerusalem and Judah, everyone to his city" (Nehemiah 7:5-6).

> **Reclaim your history, and you reclaim your story. There are promises in your family line, and inheritances for you.**

The scripture goes on to list the number of men who returned from each clan, as they identified themselves with the spiritual history of their family lines. By the end of chapter 7, this information was used to settle the people in their respective cities, according to their ancestry.

The point?

Reclaim your history, and you reclaim your story. There are promises in your family line, and inheritances for you. Though you may have been in a type of "exile," rediscover and reconnect with what God WANTS to do through your family line and decide that the exile ends with you.

You are going Home.

GOD HAS A CALENDAR

Now comes an incredibly dramatic part of this already dramatic story.

Under the direction of Ezra, the scribe who was part of the company that had returned, the people brought forth the Book of the Law (the Torah), from which Ezra read publicly for many hours before all the people.

This event was a remarkable restoration of a specific commandment of God in the Torah, dating back to the days of Moses.

> *And Moses commanded them, saying: "At the end of every seven years, at the appointed time in the year of release, at the Feast of Tabernacles, when all Israel comes to appear before the Lord your God in the place which He chooses, you shall read this law before all Israel in their hearing. Gather the people together, men and women and little ones, and the stranger who is within your gates, that they may hear and that they may learn to fear the Lord your God and carefully observe all the words of this law, and that their children, who have not known it, may hear and learn to fear the Lord your God as long as you live in the land which you cross the Jordan to possess"* (Deuteronomy 31:10-13).

Nehemiah 8:2 tells us that this intentional returning, corporately, to the Word of God began on the first day of the seventh month of the year, the final days leading up to the biblically appointed time of the Feast of Tabernacles. As a people, those in Nehemiah's company likely had not heard the Torah (Bible) read to them in this way in a generation or more. As they corporately gathered, heard, and received the Word, they remembered who they were. They began to understand and fully discover once again their mandate as a people before God, in carrying out the words of the Law, including the observance of the Feasts of the Lord.

Nehemiah had already instituted the use of the trumpet *(shofar)* as a means to rally the people together to prepare for battle: "Wherever you hear the sound of the trumpet, rally to us there. Our God will fight for us" (4:20). Now the blowing of the shofar took on a whole new level of significance.

DID YOU KNOW?

Kingly Genealogy: According to Matthew 1, the genealogy of Jesus Christ is represented in this general period of Israel's history by King Jehoiachin and his uncle King Zedekiah, the last two kings of Judah—who were both literally carried away from Jerusalem into captivity in Babylon.

The very day that they began to read from the Book of the Law was, amazingly, by the sovereignty of God, the day of the Feast of Trumpets (Leviticus 23:23-25), which is today known as Rosh Hashanah and signals the beginning of a New Year on the Jewish civil calendar! The sound of the shofar is used prominently at the Feast of Trumpets (Rosh Hashanah) as a call to assembly, to repentance, and to introspection in the "Ten Days of Awe," leading up to the Day of Atonement on Yom Kippur.

This return to the Torah took place just as the period of these Fall feasts, the holiest days of the year, were about to begin. Through their reading of the Law (8:14), they discovered the biblical commands regarding the Feast of Tabernacles, which was about to begin on the biblical calendar, including the command to dwell in booths *(sukkot)* during the feast. When this became clear, through the rediscovery and re-reading of the Word, they determined together that they should immediately make preparations for the restoration of this biblical holiday in the way that God had commanded them to observe it as a people.

It was through their reading of the Word of God that their identity as a people was clarified once again. See the elements at work together here:

- The Word of God

- The corporate gathering and receiving of the Word

- In the land of their inheritance

- In alignment with the biblical calendar.

What things in our time, in our day, are becoming "clear" again, as we read the Word of God with fresh eyes and rediscover our call to biblical culture and practice?

Powerfully, the people of Judah had returned to rebuild the walls just in time for the days of the Fall feasts, which throughout Israel's history have been an "appointed time" as one of the three pilgrimage feast celebrations of the year—for which all Israel would come up to Jerusalem to celebrate together. Now, the people were assembled in the city of Jerusalem, right on time to meet with God as a corporate nation, as His calendar commanded them.

The way in which the Feast of Tabernacles celebration was restored just as they rebuilt the walls of the city was sovereign and miraculous!

The scripture says that the joyful observance of these celebrations had not been experienced in such a way since the days of Joshua:

So the whole assembly of those who had returned from the captivity made booths and sat under the booths; for since the days of Joshua the son of Nun until that day the children of Israel had not done so. And there was very great gladness (Nehemiah 8:17).

As they celebrated the biblical calendar once again for the first time in decades, God empowered them to rebuild the spiritual walls of their nation even as they literally rebuilt the physical walls of Jerusalem as watchmen.

But here is the question for you. Do you realize that this kind of biblical alignment is happening today? Miraculous, global, historic, covenantal alignment—in our day and time!

In the present day, there is a striking parallel to this occurrence. All around the world, there is an awakening of "Jerusalem-based Christianity," a Christianity that understands itself in connection to

Jesus, Yeshua, and His Jewish identity. For example, there is the modern Christian celebration of the Feast of Tabernacles. Around the world, simultaneous to the awakening of the Christian community to our biblical roots through reading and rediscovering the Word of God, Christians have come up to Zion every year since 1980 as spiritual Watchmen on the Wall. This began through the work of the early leaders of the International Christian Embassy Jerusalem and is continued on today through many different ministries, calling out to the global Church and calling out to YOU to come into alignment with God's covenantal realities.

Likewise, the Day of Prayer for the Peace of Jerusalem is now observed by millions all around the world on the first Sunday of every October (daytopray.com). Truly there is great joy in keeping the biblical feasts, which are God's feasts (Leviticus 23:2), and in coming into alignment with His land, His ancient people the Jews, and His biblical calendar.

The Church is coming "out of exile" and "returning home" to our spiritual Home, Jerusalem. We are corporately "hearing the word of the Lord" again as a people and coming into alignment with our true identity as worshippers of the God of Israel. You are a part of this return from exile. Your story is connected to His story. History.

RESTORING THE TABERNACLE OF DAVID

Another dimension of this spiritual restoration was Nehemiah's recognizing and restoring the heart of worship expressed through David and Solomon—rebuilding the walls so that the spirit of the

Tabernacle of David and Temple worship could be established again. This is, of course, the ultimate destiny of Jerusalem... to be the capital city of Worship for the world.

David, known throughout the generations as "a man after God's own heart" (1 Samuel 13:14), was the leader who instituted night-and-day worship in the Tabernacle in Jerusalem. He purposed in his heart that worship of the God of Israel would be the central characteristic of his kingdom. God in turn promised that David's house would endure forever (2 Samuel 7:16).

Although David did not build the Temple—that was carried out by his son Solomon, at the command of the Lord—it was David's desire that was later fulfilled in the next generation to build a permanent house for God in Jerusalem (2 Samuel 7:12-13). Perhaps it is due to David's commitment to God's will that the Temple is remembered as King David's. As the prophet Amos says, "On that day I will raise up the tabernacle of David, which has fallen down, and repair its damages; I will raise up its ruins, and rebuild it as in the days of old" (Amos 9:11).

Like the life of David, God wants to start something in you, something that continues in and through your biological and spiritual children. God wants to give you an inter-generational dream.

When Jerusalem was destroyed by the Babylonians, it seemed that the Temple was lost forever in the ruins of the city. But those who came back to rebuild the city of Jerusalem were part of God's plan to bring about the Second Temple period, propelled forward by the leadership of Nehemiah, Zerubbabel, Ezra, and the prophets Haggai and Zechariah.

God was not looking for a rebuilt city; He was looking for restored worship from a restored people.

When the walls of the city were rebuilt, one of the first things that Nehemiah put in place, like David of years past, was worship in the temple area, according to the biblical practices of the Tabernacle of David and Solomon's Temple.

Nehemiah 9 is devoted to these declarations of worship brought forth by the Levites, in this time of the Fall feasts being observed.

Chapter 10 shows the conscious decision of Nehemiah's leadership to establish worship once again as central in Jerusalem:

For the children of Israel and the children of Levi shall bring the offering of the grain, of the new wine and the oil, to the storerooms where the articles of the sanctuary are, where the priests who minister and the gatekeepers and the singers are; and we will not neglect the house of our God (Nehemiah 10:39, emphasis added).

Nehemiah purposed in his heart that offerings of worship would be of utmost priority within the rebuilt walls, and that they would not neglect God's house in this season of fulfillment of the promise.

God was not looking for a rebuilt city; He was looking for restored worship from a restored people.

HISTORY ON THE WALLS

Now comes perhaps the crowning moment... the dedication of the wall of Jerusalem.

Now at the dedication of the wall of Jerusalem they sought out the Levites in all their places, to bring them to Jerusalem to celebrate the dedication with gladness, both with thanksgivings and singing, with cymbals and stringed instruments and harps (12:27).

Nehemiah literally brought the leaders of Judah on top of the wall to oversee the dedication as he then appointed two large thanksgiving choirs (v. 31) to journey in worship literally on the walls as they were rebuilt.

When I bring our pilgrimage groups to Jerusalem, one of the most meaningful experiences we have is the "Ramparts Walk," where I bring our groups up a winding staircase inside of Jaffa Gate, up to the top of the literal walls of the Old City. We then begin to walk on the rampart walls of the Old City, praying and singing as we go, and occasionally, blowing a shofar. The last time I was there, we encountered another group of Dutch and German intercessors who said that they have had a group of people on the walls EVERY DAY in intercession for the past 15 years. What is happening? Something is sweeping through the body of Christ (the body of

Messiah) in the nations of the earth, as a prophetic people discern, just like Nehemiah did, that it is time to return Home.

Through actions such as these, we can clearly see the priority that Nehemiah placed on Davidic worship being restored to the city of Jerusalem. In this atmosphere, the singers rejoiced and sang loudly, together with all the people, and thanksgiving rang through the air of Jerusalem, "so that the joy of Jerusalem was heard afar off" (12:43).

Nehemiah, though he was just one man, stepped into the reality of the Davidic call, so that worship would be restored in Jerusalem, and so that much later an entire generation of Israelite descendants would see the restoration of Israel as a sovereign nation in 1948. And because of his courage and commitment to follow the heart of God in his generation, Nehemiah helped to pave the way for many generations of Jews and Christians to step into the call of standing in the gap as watchmen on behalf of the land.

By his life and example, Nehemiah became an initial fulfillment of the promises to David; and a forerunner of Jesus, of the Jewish rebuilders of modern Israel, and of future Christian Zionists—all of whom would be part of the restoration of Israel.

As a wall builder, when you reconnect to the rootedness that comes from alignment with God's calendar and His people, your identity is fortified in God's eternal foundations, and you are able to rebuild with a strength that cannot be thwarted by attacks from the enemies of God.

When you reconnect to the rootedness that comes from alignment with God's calendar and His people, your identity is fortified in God's eternal foundations.

The powers of darkness have never been able to withstand God's eternal covenant that He made with His people and His land. Out of the ashes and against all odds, the people of Israel returned to their ancestral homeland, led by the supernatural power of God that intervened in human history.

Nehemiah's day was a powerful beginning to the restoration story that God was telling. Many more trials were ahead for the people of Israel and an even more widespread Diaspora into the nations of the world. The Second Temple would even be destroyed by the Romans in 70 AD.

Even as the persecution intensified throughout the centuries and continues in various forms to this day, the waves of restoration would grow ever stronger as God engineered and engineers the fulfillment of the promise. The story of Nehemiah proves that God has a calendar that He keeps, even now as then, within the borders of a specific land (Israel) and a specific city (Jerusalem), through a specific people (the Jews) to include "whosoever will" (the nations).

FOR FURTHER STUDY:

1. How does your personal "rebuilding" connect to the rebuilding of those around you in your church, city, or community?

_____

_____

_____

_____

_____

_____

_____

2. What is one positive, defining characteristic of your family roots and identity?

_____

_____

_____

_____

_____

3. If you are a believer in the God of the Bible, have you considered how your biblical, Jewish roots impact your daily life today? How can you actively apply this truth to your life now?

_____

_____

_____

_____

_____

_____

4. As we have studied together, the rebuilding project of Nehemiah was focused on the city of Jerusalem. What role does Jerusalem play (or should it play) in your personal faith and rebuilding? What would it mean for you to be a "watchman on the wall" for Jerusalem?

_____

_____

_____

_____

_____

CHAPTER 10

THE ULTIMATE BATTLE

WORSHIPPING YOUR WAY TO VICTORY

"The battle line between good and evil runs through the heart of every man."

– Aleksandr Solzhenitsyn
Russian novelist and gulag survivor[19]

Throughout history, the people of God, both Jew and Gentile, have faced heavy battles and intense oppositions in every generation. Beginning with the Jews, Joshua and the battle of Jericho. David and the Philistines. Esther and the evil plot by Haman. Roman oppression against Jews and Christians. The Crusades, Inquisitions, and Pogroms that relentlessly attacked the Jews... leading up to the horrors of the Holocaust. And in recent years, the intense persecutions against Christians in Nigeria, Sudan, China, North Korea. The mass exodus of Christians from the Arab Middle East in the last several decades. And the list goes on...

With all the oppositions that the people of God have faced, it is crucial that we remember the ultimate battle we are engaged in.

> **The ultimate battle is the battle over worship.**

ONE FIGHT

Amidst the many battles and skirmishes confronting God's people throughout the centuries, there is only one ultimate battle that is raging, and that battle's outcome cannot be negotiated by heads of nations or settled in international courts. It can only be won with Heaven's resources and with the yielding of our hearts.

That ultimate battle is the battle over worship. The individual worship of the heart, and the combined worship of a corporate covenantal people.

This is the battle that you are engaged in as you seek to live as a wall builder in this hour, calling on the God of Abraham, Isaac, Jacob... and Nehemiah.

As much as the global media today would try to say otherwise, the true battle is not about land settlements or social justice or even racial equality. It is about covenant, and God will never rescind the covenant promises He made to His people. Not in Nehemiah's day, and not in the hour in which we currently live. Covenant is the agency through which God moves in history. The "nations can rage" and the "kings of the earth can conspire together," but God, who sits in Heaven, is still laughing at their plans (see Psalm 2).

The enemy hates the covenants of God, because they are an eternal indictment against him and they cannot be shaken by any evil attack. But even though the outcome of the eternal battle has already been decided, Satan rages all the more against God and His people. Scripture says, "He is filled with fury, because he knows that his time is short" (Revelation 12:12). The

> **Covenant is the agency through which God moves in history.**

ultimate battle has many battle fronts—everything from terrorism to media wars to the content of elementary school textbooks—but all those fronts lead back to the question of *who* will be worshipped in Jerusalem: God, or some manifestation or form of the enemy.

This is the ultimate question that affects the administration of the entire planet, and with it the nature of our lives on a daily basis.

ONE EPICENTER

When I first visited the Temple Mount area in Jerusalem, I was awestruck that I was standing in the very location where Abraham went to offer his son Isaac, where Solomon's Temple had stood, and where Nehemiah and the Jewish exiles returned to rebuild many years after being taken to Assyria and Babylon. I was also overwhelmed with the awareness that this spot is where the godly worship of the nations is beginning to converge at this very hour, as Gentile believers in the God of Israel from the nations increasingly stream up to Jerusalem year after year, in direct fulfillment of numerous biblical prophecies. This is the place where Messiah will reign and bring Shalom to the nations of the earth.

As the epicenter of the battle between good and evil on planet Earth, the Temple Mount has been the subject of negotiation after negotiation in an attempt to secure an enduring peace. Whether we fully realize it or not, these realities affect each of us who call on the God of Israel for salvation, because God has commissioned each of us to earnestly seek the peace of Jerusalem:

You who call on the Lord,
  give yourselves no rest,
and give him no rest till he establishes Jerusalem
  and makes her the praise of the earth (Isaiah 62:6b-7, NIV, emphasis added).

Please note that this does not say, "You Jews, who call on the Lord..." or, "those of you with an interest in Israel, who call on the Lord..."

No, it is clear. The mandate is for all of us.

This mandate is for you, if you call yourself a believer. It is not described as optional.

If we are going to CALL on the God of the Bible for salvation, for covenant, for meaning in our lives, then we have a responsibility along with that call, and that is to enter into His heavenly, inter-generational, and ultimate plan for Jerusalem.

Why would God be so insistent on this instruction to us, that He would tell us to "give Him no rest" until this assignment is complete? I believe it is because everything that happens in

Jerusalem has a direct impact on the rest of the world. How often do you see a "World" section of a news publication that doesn't include some mention of Jerusalem or the Middle East conflict? Jerusalem is a plumb line, a "True North." How we discern, connect with, prioritize, and align with Jerusalem—individually and as people groups—is both a sign of where we are in our spiritual journey, and also, scripture hints, a central point that impacts our eternal destiny.

DID YOU KNOW?

Anointed Gentile: The Persian king Cyrus the Great, who first allowed the people of Judah to return to Jerusalem, is the only Gentile in the Old Testament who bears the title of being "anointed" by God (Isaiah 45:1). In modern times, President Harry S. Truman identified himself with the Persian ruler, saying "I am Cyrus," about his pledge of support for the new state of Israel in 1948.

In Joel 3, God says that there will come a time when He will enter into judgment with the nations who oppose His people Israel and divide up His Land:

For behold, in those days and at that time, When I bring back the captives of Judah and Jerusalem, I will also gather all nations, And bring them down to the Valley of Jehoshaphat; And I will enter into judgment with them there On account of My people, My heritage Israel, Whom they have scattered among the nations; They have also divided up My land (Joel 3:1-2).

Conversely, in Isaiah 56, God says that great blessing will come to those who stand with His people Israel:

Also the sons of the foreigner Who join themselves to the Lord, to serve Him, And to love the name of the Lord, to be His servants— Everyone who keeps from defiling the Sabbath, And holds fast My covenant—Even them I will bring to My holy mountain, And make them joyful in My house of prayer. Their burnt offerings and their sacrifices Will be accepted on My altar; For My house shall be called a house of prayer for all nations (Isaiah 56:6-7).

Jerusalem is the absolute geographic center of our faith, both the birth of our faith in the crucifixion, resurrection, and Day of Pentecost outpouring, and our future hope, when Messiah will return and reign from the throne of David in Jerusalem. We will not see the fullness of God's Kingdom on earth without the fulfillment of the promises that God has spoken over that city—which involve Jerusalem being what scripture calls "the praise of the earth," and her serving as the host location of the fullness of worship of the God of Israel.

Jerusalem is the center focus of the entire world. This is not a mistake; it is part of God's plan. "Thus says the Lord God: 'This is Jerusalem; I have set her in the midst of the nations and the countries all around her'" (Ezekiel 5:5).

It is shocking to consider that in the midst of this global battle of epic proportions, in many cases we as the Church have been completely and totally unaware of the reality of the spiritual warfare that we are in. Surrounded by the comforts of a thinly protected freedom (at least in the Western Church), we have been caught up in trivial theological disputes and insulated distractions that ultimately have no bearing on the advance of God's Kingdom.

In this crucial time of history, we need to be those who, like Nehemiah, understand that the time is NOW to rebuild our broken-down walls, resting upon the rock-solid foundation of God's covenant. We can and must be part of building the walls that God intends for us to build—in truth and righteousness.

Will you follow the call and example of Nehemiah? Will you care? Will you pray, and then become the answer to that prayer? Will you be a wall builder in your life, and in your generation?

ONE PEOPLE

The enemy may not be able to make you turn your back on God, but he knows that if he can DISTRACT you just enough from what

> **Worship is one of the great keys, and indeed the doorway, to coming into the wholeness that God intends for His people!**

God intends, he will achieve his purpose. He knows that as long as you remain distanced from the battle or distracted in the midst of it, he will make you ineffective as a soldier in the army of God.

This is why it is so vital that we partner with God and others to rebuild the Broken Places in our lives. Your healing in your soul and personal relationships is not just about you! When you experience God restoring your soul, your relationships, or supernaturally resurrecting your broken dreams, you begin to become a worshipper and a wall builder who makes an impact on those around you—strengthening others by your relationship with them.

Worship is one of the great keys, and indeed the doorway, to coming into the wholeness that God intends for His people!

I have heard it said, and I believe it is absolutely true, that you become like *what* or *whom* you worship. Indeed, scripture tells us, "We shall be like Him, for we shall see Him as He is" (1 John 3:2). Please note, we become like Him when we see Him as He IS, not as we have made Him to be. It is only when we see, we behold more of God's reality, His greatness, His character, His holiness, His other-ness that is so beyond our natural understanding, that we are then transformed, glory to glory, into that likeness.

As we worship God consistently from the heart, we begin to grow in God's characteristics, which are the fruit of His Holy Spirit. If you find someone who is on the pathway to healing, freedom, and wholeness,

> **The personal battle of repairing Broken Places in our lives is absolutely connected to the ultimate battle of light versus darkness.**

that person is almost always a growing worshipper.

Whether it is expressed in your own personal breakthrough, or in being part of the global movement of watchmen on the walls of Jerusalem, the enemy hates your worship! The personal battle of repairing Broken Places in our lives is absolutely connected to the ultimate battle of light versus darkness, of good versus evil. And in that battle, we can only rise in victory as high as our worship rises.

We must, like Nehemiah, rebuild the walls of righteousness in our generation. We must focus on what is important and essential. Psalm 16:8 says, "I have set the Lord always before me." We must live our lives through the prism of the God of history, the God of the Bible, the God of Israel, prioritizing what He calls us to prioritize. As a people worshipping through difficulties to find wholeness in our personal lives, and linked together through committed relationships, we become representatives of a greater reality that the enemy can't touch. This is how we rebuild the walls in our day.

Over and over, Nehemiah had reasons to give up. The journey itself was dangerous and hard. The enemies of Israel attacked his character and opposed him. Then Judah and the other Jews—the very people he was trying to help—turned against him. Nehemiah had reasons to become offended and to become bitter. And if he had, he would have aborted his mission and purpose.

God is looking for a people who have made the decision, through a lifestyle of surrendered worship, that they will be unoffendable in this hour. In other words, blessed are the flexible, for they shall not be broken! Like Nehemiah, you WILL face opposition; painful, repeated, frustrating opposition. It will come from those you trusted. It will hurt. But if your heart is secured in the Lord, you will not be moved by these wounds.

If we become firmly planted with our roots going deep into the soil of the Word of God and His purposes for this hour, He can use us to make a greater impact that will remain. We will become a value added wherever we are, because we have made the daily choice to make our lives count in the ultimate battle of worship.

WALL BUILDERS AT WAR

If there is anything we can glean from the story of Nehemiah it is this: God is looking for committed, courageous wall builders. We are not here to simply fill a pew on Sunday morning; we are not here to be churchgoers; we are not here to have a nice local church. We are at war, contending in this generation, and in every generation, for the purposes of God!

War has been declared on your family... war has been declared on your destiny... and war has been declared on your city and nation. Whether or not you are cognizant of it, there are

> **We are at war, contending in this generation, and in every generation, for the purposes of God!**

destructive forces at work in this world that want to destroy you, take you out, and take you down.

Just as we see in the pages of Nehemiah, this reality is the story of the Jewish people through the centuries. The testimony of the Jews is of a people who endure even in the midst of suffering— when things are *not* as they should be. What we learn from the Jewish people, in the midst of the battles they have faced, is that the only thing that matters in this world is an enduring connectedness to the God who calls things that are not as though they were (Romans 4:17).

In God's eternal perspective, the righteous walls of truth and justice exist in the heavenly reality, even though they have not yet been fully built in the earth. God knows the outcome of these things before they appear in the natural. He is OUTSIDE of time and already knows what is going to happen long before it does, and before man begins to move in the foreordained purpose that He has established.

As He said to the young prophet Jeremiah, "Before I formed you in the womb I knew you, before you were born I set you apart; I appointed you as a prophet to the nations" (Jeremiah 1:5). God is looking for those who will partner with Him in what He desires to do. To worship through our battles is to partner with God in declaring the heavenly realities of His Kingdom in the middle of earthly circumstances. It is how we "increase His government" (Isaiah 9:7) in the here and now.

As the battle rages on, neutrality in this hour is not an option.

What would have happened if Nehemiah had stayed in Persia?

Can you imagine?

History hinged on his decision.

I promise you, more history hinges on your decisions than you realize.

Leave exile.

Journey to Zion.

Rebuild the walls.

FOR FURTHER STUDY:

1. Do you see your personal worship as a weapon for spiritual battle? Why or why not?

_____

_____

_____

_____

_____

2. Describe a time in your life when your personal engagement in worship was key to finding healing in a broken area of your life. What did you learn from it?

_____

_____

_____

_____

_____

_____

_____

3. Are you willing to become the answer to the prayers that you pray? How can you make this type of lifestyle action become an expression of your worship?

_____

_____

_____

_____

_____

4. In what ways in your present life circumstances can you choose today to be a wall builder?

_____

_____

_____

_____

_____

HISTORICAL TIMELINE

1010-970 BC: King David reigns in Israel.

970-931 BC: King Solomon reigns in Israel.

931 BC: The kingdom is divided into Israel (north) and Judah (south), at beginning of the reign of Rehoboam, son of Solomon.

722 BC: Fall of Israel (northern kingdom) to Assyria.

715-686 BC: King Hezekiah reigns in righteousness in Judah; however, he opens the treasures of his kingdom to envoys from Babylon.

640-609 BC: King Josiah reigns in Judah, bringing extensive religious reforms.

597 BC: First group of captives is taken from Judah to Babylon.

590s—530s BC: Daniel prophesies during the reign of Babylonians, Medes, and Persians in Babylon, up until his death in the days of the Persian (Achaemenid) Empire.

587-586 BC: Siege of Jerusalem by the Babylonians.

586 BC: Jerusalem is destroyed by fire, majority of Judah taken into exile.

559-530 BC: Cyrus II (Cyrus the Great) reigns in Persia.

539 BC: Babylon conquered by Medes and Persians.

538 BC: Cyrus the Great commissions the first group of exiles to return to Judah, under the leadership of Zerubbabel.

522-486 BC: Darius I reigns in Persia.

516 BC: Second Temple (initial rebuilding) is completed in Jerusalem.

486-465 BC: Xerxes I (Ahasuerus) reigns in Persia, where Esther (Hadassah) served as queen.

465-424 BC: Artaxerxes I reigns in Persia, where Nehemiah served as cupbearer.

445 BC: Nehemiah travels back to Jerusalem.

445 BC: Walls of Jerusalem are completed under Nehemiah; the Feast of Tabernacles is celebrated in Jerusalem.

Please note that the exact dates of many events listed above are debated by scholars of ancient history. This representation is intended to point readers toward generally accepted dates of major historical benchmarks to give context for our study of Nehemiah.

REFERENCES

http://www.biblicalarchaeologytruth.com/nehemiahs-wall.html

ENDNOTES:

[1] https://www.mentalfloss.com/article/63389/roosevelts-man-arena

[2] https://www.inspiringquotes.us/author/7313-david-ben-gurion

[3] https://www.imdb.com/title/tt0234215/characters/nm0048127

[4] https://aish.com/the_history_of_hatikvah/

[5] https://www.quotemaster.org/building+the+future

[6] http://www.quotationspage.com/quote/37976.html

[7] https://www.successories.com/iquote/author/3800/viktor-e-frankl-quotes/1

[8] https://www.goodreads.com/quotes/332507-in-essentials-unity-in-non-essentials-liberty-in-all-things-charity

[9] https://www.cbsnews.com/news/the-man-who-stopped-the-tsunami/

[10] https://www.bbcamerica.com/blogs/50-%09churchill-%09quotes--49128

[11] https://www.brainyquote.com/quotes/georg_buchner_394527?src=t_halfway

[12] https://www.thegrowthfaculty.com/blog/topquotesatomichabits

[13] https://www.history.com/topics/american-revolution/valley-forge

[14] https://www.media-marketing.com/en/news/want-go-fast-go-alone-want-go-far-go-together-african-proverb

[15] https://thelehrhaus.com/scholarship/as-one-person-with-one-heart-misunderstood-in-unison

[16] https://www.kevinhalloran.net/best-c-s-lewis-quotes

[17] https://www.etymonline.com/word/cult

[18] https://www.etymonline.com/word/culture

[19] https://www.bartleby.com/essay/Aleksandr-Solzhenitsyn-The-Battleline-Between-Good-And-PK7LLHQ5U3D5

ABOUT THE AUTHOR

Bishop **Robert Stearns** is the founder and executive director of Eagles' Wings, a dynamic relational ministry involved in a variety of outreaches and strategic projects around the world. He has ministered in more than 30 nations around the world, with a central focus on the nation of Israel.

A powerful communicator, Robert Stearns is the author of eight books, and speaks around the country at various churches, conferences, and venues. Robert is also an accomplished recording artist and soloist, with performances in the U.S., Europe, and Israel, including both the prestigious Carnegie Hall and St. Patrick's Cathedral in New York City.

Robert is the visionary of the worldwide prayer initiative, "The Day of Prayer for the Peace of Jerusalem," which is observed annually on the first Sunday of October, and has the participation of over 500,000 churches in over 175 nations.

Robert is also the presiding Bishop of the historic Tabernacle church in Buffalo, NY and President of the Israel Christian Nexus in Los Angeles, CA. He is at the forefront of educating Christian communities worldwide regarding the role of Israel, the Jewish people, and our shared Judeo-Christian values; and in 2020 was named among the top 50 Christian Allies of Israel by the Israel Allies Foundation. Joining the ranks of some of the world's top leaders such as Ambassador John Bolton, Caroline Glick, and Alan Dershowitz, Robert received the 2021 "Genesis Award" for his courageous leadership and deep love for Israel.

For additional information about Eagles' Wings Ministries or to book Robert Stearns for an event, visit eagleswings.org.

Subscribe and follow Robert Stearns:

Instagram: @RobertRStearns

YouTube: /RobertStearns

Facebook: @RobertRStearns (Public Figure)

PAY IT FORWARD

Thank you for embarking on Nehemiah's journey with me. My prayer is that you will be able to rise and rebuild in your own life.

The power of a good book lies not just in its words but in its lasting impact on its readers.

If you've been touched, inspired, or transformed by *Rise and Rebuild*, I invite you to share your thoughts and experiences by writing an Amazon review.

Feel free to keep it simple and share from your heart. When joined by others, the power of a single positive review has the remarkable ability to spread this message like wildfire, touching countless lives along the way.

Your support means the world to me.

—Bishop Robert Stearns

You can leave a review by visiting:
https://www.amazon.com/review/create-review/listing

ENDORSEMENTS

Bishop Robert Stearns is a unique individual with an unusual call on his life to help us understand the importance of the nation of Israel for our world. I have witnessed and been part of the important work of Eagles' Wings and its global impact. I urge you to read Robert's book, absorb it, and implement these valuable lessons from Nehemiah's story in your own life today.

—Mike Huckabee
Former Governor of Arkansas

Robert Stearns' excellent book, "Rise and Rebuild," is sure to cause a renaissance of hope in people who have suffered, been disappointed, and simply lost the heart to believe that they can start again. I found myself refreshed and renewed as I read it.

—Cindy Jacobs
Co-founder, Generals International

Personal tragedy, loss, and failed dreams visit everyone on the planet at some time in their lives. These devastating events can make us or break us. They can be stumbling blocks or stepping stones. It is possible for our darkest days to be followed by our most brilliant. The outcome is dependent for the most part on our perspective.

Bishop Robert Stearns has authentic personal testimony confirming how one can stand in the midst of fierce opposition and brutal attack, and gloriously rebuild what has been lost or weakened in the assault. His book, "Rise and Rebuild," will infuse you with faith, hope, and courage as you read through the profound revelations, insights, and teachings it contains. This is a timely book for this hour as we call for lives, families, regions, and nations to embrace the journey and process designed by the Lord — a journey that creates breakthrough and glorious eternal testimony.

—Dr. Patricia King
Author, Minister, Influencer
www.patriciaking.com

Jesus is the great Restorer. He is the crucified and risen Lord of Glory who embodies the defeat over pain and death. I am so glad that Robert Stearns is offering God's people hope in Lord, in the midst of challenges that life presents us all.

I deeply appreciate Robert's heart to serve the people of God in this area. It is my prayer that every reader will run into the arms of Jesus and trust Him to be their deliverance and eternal victory.

—Michael Koulianos
Founder, Jesus Image

How can one find opportunities for hope, faith and renewal amid the many challenges of a broken world? Two and a half millennia ago, Nehemiah showed us the blueprint. And in our age—an era of prophetic wonders coming to pass before our very eyes—the story of Nehemiah's return home from exile to the Land of Israel has taken on even more imminent significance.

There is a great need for fresh attention to this gripping, inspiring Biblical story. Fortunately, Bishop Robert Stearns—a master teacher and extraordinary leader—has provided that very thing. This book is sure to become essential reading for those who seek to understand their own lives in the context of this wonderful, understudied Biblical work.

—Rabbi Dr. Ari Lamm
CEO of Bnai Zion

My good friend Bishop Robert Stearns is without question at the forefront of what God is doing in the world today, both in Israel and in nations far and wide.

In this his latest book, "Rise and Rebuild," Robert offers powerful insights from the biblical account of Nehemiah that will give you the courage and strength you need to be all that God has called you to be.

—Robert Morris

Senior Pastor, Gateway Church

Bestselling Author of *The Blessed Life, Beyond Blessed,* and *The God I Never Knew*

Thank you, Bishop Stearns, for reclaiming the inspirational and under-appreciated story of Nehemiah. A great rabbi once taught me, 'You can preach like most prophets or you can rebuild a city like Nehemiah!' This essential text is a powerful guide to rebuild and to be rebuilt; stronger, wiser, and more loving as a people and as a person in God's image.

—Rabbi Jonah Dov Pesner

Director, The Religious Action Center

There has never been a time in our world when the need for effective tools to address adversity has been greater. Thankfully, my friend Dr. Robert Stearns has penned an empowering guide based on time-tested principles that will enable you to rise above even the most challenging of circumstances, to rebuild what was broken and triumphantly cross the finish line of your life's mission.

Breakthrough and victory await you within these pages.

—Touré Roberts
Bestselling Author, Entrepreneur, and Pastor

"Rise and Rebuild" is a rallying cry for every believer to step into their divine destiny and to become unoffendable, courageous, and committed in the face of challenges. It reminds us that ordinary lives can become extraordinary vessels in God's hands, bringing healing and restoration to a broken world. Bishop Robert Stearns encourages us all to embrace worship as a lifestyle, an expression of faith, and a powerful weapon in spiritual battles.

I highly recommend "Rise and Rebuild" to every believer seeking to overcome the obstacles in your life and the scoffers who want to hinder you from fulfilling your destiny. Whether you are new to faith or a seasoned believer, this book will inspire you to rebuild the walls of faith in your generation and beyond. Let it ignite a fresh passion for worship and empower you to embrace your divine calling as a modern-day Nehemiah.

—Gordon Robertson
President, The Christian Broadcasting Network

Bishop Robert Stearns is one of the leading influencers of this generation, pioneering the increasingly vital and irreplaceable relationship between Christians and Jews, extending to the Muslim community and all people of goodwill. His new book on the life of Nehemiah is a truly inspirational work that will strengthen and shape this growing dialogue of common faith and common fate. I highly recommend Bishop Stearns' exemplary and prayerful message of hope, "Rise and Rebuild."

—Rabbi Marc Schneier
Founding Rabbi, The Hampton Synagogue
President, the Foundation for Ethnic Understanding

Dr. Stearns takes you on a journey to the crossroads of biblical revelation, contemporary reality, and practical application, where he places you before an ever-changing kaleidoscope of the changing colors of the challenges of your life. You will see you as you were, as you are, and as you can become. You will never see you the same. He invites you into the shop of the Master Builder. He will reveal your struggle to follow the divine design of the Architect of the universe. He will remind you of both the battles of building a life and reflecting on the divine design in the mind of God that always leads to His glory.

—Kenneth C. Ulmer, DMin, PhD
Senior Advisor to the President for Community Reconciliation
Biola University

The book of Nehemiah, which in his compelling book Robert Stearns deepens and actualizes for the believer's current existence, witnesses to God's power in gathering his people and granting them a new beginning in the land of Israel after the tragedy of exile. It addresses questions as relevant as ever for both Jews and Christians, such as how to rebuild God's house when it is in ruins.

These and many other issues the author addresses: they unite Jews and Christians in a world in which they are increasingly called to renew their faith, walking together toward the heavenly Jerusalem in a relationship of friendship and mutual respect, in which Robert Stearns is one of the most active protagonists of our time.

—Fr. Francesco Giosù Voltaggio
Neocatechumenal Way, Jerusalem, Israel

My friend, Robert Stearns is a builder! In his new book, Rise and Rebuild, Robert takes us on a journey through the book of Nehemiah and shares eternal lessons he has experienced. If something is broken in your life or God is calling you to rebuild your family, ministry, or the lives of others, you will be blessed by this book. I am excited about and say yes to this clarion call for all of us to Rise and Rebuild!

—Dr. Billy Wilson
Oral Roberts University President
Empowered21 Global Chair
Pentecostal World Fellowship Chair

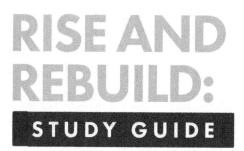

RISE AND REBUILD:

STUDY GUIDE

THE TIME IS NOW...

The *Rise and Rebuild Study Guide* is your transformative companion to help you discover your full potential as a rebuilder in the Kingdom of God. Echoing the clarion call of Nehemiah, this guide is an essential tool for those seeking to overcome any obstacle.

Designed to complement each chapter of Robert Stearns' *Rise and Rebuild* book as well as the bonus video materials, this study guide invites you to delve deeper through thought-provoking questions for practical application to help rise and rebuild in every area of life.

RISE AND REBUILD

Whether you're gathering in small groups for a weekly study or pursuing personal growth through self-study, this guide is a powerful resource for personal application to fulfill God's plans and purposes for your life.

Experience a rich and interactive engagement with the teachings, taking a moment to reflect on and expand your insights. With prayers for life-altering transformations, this guide is not just a manual but a journey of personal growth and blessing.

AVAILABLE AT

Did You Receive Your Bonuses Yet?

When you purchased your *Rise and Rebuild* book,
Did you know that it came with these exclusive bonuses?

RiseandRebuildBook.com

Visit the website above to receive the following bonuses absolutely FREE!

52-Day Blueprint: The ultimate bonus for *Rise and Rebuild,* download this 52-day devotional to accompany your book.

10-part Video Book Study: Watch excerpts of Robert teaching as he reflects on each chapter, filmed on location in Israel.

Wall Builders Checklist: This checklist helps you identify areas in your own life that need to be rebuilt.

Discover Eagles' Wings

Robert Stearns founded Eagles' Wings in 1994, sparking a global movement to advance three biblical mandates:

LOVE ISRAEL

Actively praying and working for lasting peace in Israel.

GROW COMMUNITY

Renewing spiritual community around the world.

BUILD BRIDGES

Fostering understanding across cultural divides.

Learn more and respond to the call at

eagleswings.org